APPROACHES TO 'A' LEVEL
HISTORY 1789–1871

KING'S SCHOOL, ELY

Pupil's Name	Value	Date Purchased	Master's Signature	Office Use only
Caroline Jackson	35p	25/9/73		

APPROACHES
TO ADVANCED LEVEL
HISTORY 1789–1871

by
BERWICK COATES, M.A.
Assistant History Master at Kingston Grammar School

ALLMAN & SON LIMITED, LONDON

First published in Great Britain 1970 by Allman and Son Limited
17-19 Foley Street, London WIA IDR

© Berwick Coates 1970

ISBN 0 204 74649 3

MADE AND PRINTED IN GREAT BRITAIN BY
THE GARDEN CITY PRESS LIMITED
LETCHWORTH, HERTFORDSHIRE

APPROACHES TO 'A' LEVEL
HISTORY 1789–1871

CONTENTS

General Introduction

This book is designed for, and addressed to, 'A' Level candidates in history.

It is set out in the form of twenty-four separate sections, each headed by a question of the type that might well appear (and in most cases has already appeared) in an 'A' Level European or Foreign History paper.

The book has two main intentions:

1. To give some guidance in the selection and organisation of material to be studied.

2. To offer some advice on the technique of writing history essays.

Whoever uses this book must be quite clear in his mind about its limitations:

it is NOT a potted history of Europe from 1789 to 1871.
it is NOT a set of 'Notes on European History'.
it is NOT a set of 'model answers'.

Reading lists are given at the end of each section. They make no claim to be exhaustive, and for the most part do not take account of scholarly articles in learned periodicals.

Scholarly articles make reading lists look impressive, but my experience is that most students ignore them, and the gifted ones find them anyway in the bibliographies of the standard authorities.

The books offered here have been chosen because they are either

easily accessible
or   readable
or   accepted as the standard authorities
     or all three.

At the end there is also a General Reading List of books which cover part or all of the whole period.

It is hoped that the book will make you think, and will help to remove from your mind the two extreme misconceptions about 'A' Level History:

1. That it is just another glorified memory test.
2. That it is a remote academic discipline of such rarefied learning and such enshrined dogmas as to be beyond the comprehension, much less the criticism and influence, of the humble student.

Finally, one point which cannot be stressed enough. This book contains many generalisations; be very wary of them. They are intended for the most part not to summarise basic truths but to provide controversial starting-points for criticism and discussion.

1 Why did a revolution break out in France in 1789?

Probably the most straightforward type of question—'Why . . ?', 'What were the reasons for . . . ?', 'What were the causes of . . . ?', and so on. In other words, a question which really *is* a question, and which requires a clear-cut answer. (Compare it with those quotations which you are so often invited to 'discuss'.)

In that sense, therefore, the question is easy, though it is appreciated that from an 'A' Level candidate's point of view the term 'easy' is a purely relative one. The difficulty, if any, is likely to come not from wondering what to say, but from deciding how to say it—a problem not of collection, but of presentation of material.

Revolutions, like wars and the fall of empires and so on, tend to have lots of causes. So, if you are to cover the ground adequately, you must do something to avoid the situation wherein you find yourself saying 'The twenty-seventh reason for the French Revolution is . . .' An essay explaining the causes of anything should not be allowed to degenerate into a list.

So group the causes. Work out some sub-headings.

For instance, all revolutions, and wars, and the decline of empires, etc., have what you call 'long-term causes' and 'short-term causes', or, if you like, 'deep-seated causes' and 'immediate causes'. Whatever way you care to express it, some causes go back a long way and some don't.

A second suggestion—a very useful one, this. It can be applied to all sorts of problems. Think of the various factors which influence historical development:

E.g. Political   Social
      Economic   Religious
      Individual personality Luck

You can probably think of more.

So the French Revolution, presumably, had some political causes, some social causes, some economic causes, and so on.

Or again, work out a sort of order of importance of your causes. Use your first page to drive home the biggest points, and employ the rest as makeweights and space-fillers. Or, if you prefer the opposite technique, save the best till last.

11

Three possible ways. You may well be able to think of more.

It doesn't really matter, within reason, what system or 'grouping' you use, as long as you avoid starting every paragraph with 'Seventhly', 'Eighthly', 'Twelfthly', etc. Different methods suit different questions. It is for you to use your common sense and (as you progress) your experience to decide which.

Why did a revolution break out?

The following factors could have a bearing on the matter, and would repay investigation.

1. The Crown	Once a symbol of unification against feudal separatism. Now heading a government centralised to a degree which killed local initiative and incentive.
	The trouble with the royal despotism established by Richelieu and Louis XIV was that it needed a series of Richelieus and Louis XIVs to run it.
	Louis XVI was no Louis XIV. His character plays a part both in the approach of revolution and in the development of the revolution.
	Similarly, the behaviour and character of Marie Antoinette (*L'Autrichienne*).
2. The nobility	The blue blood tradition which stifled talent and blocked promotion.
	Debarred from commerce (unlike its British counterpart), and so forced to rely entirely on political intrigue and maintenance of social prestige.
	Still enjoying tax immunity and feudal privilege.
	What Professor Sir Denys Brogan once called 'constitutional junk', but junk that the king and the reformers kept tripping over when they wanted to improve things.

3. The church   enjoying vast landownership
                                    huge riches
                                    social privilege
                                    tax immunity
                                    almost complete control of education.

and, perhaps because of the above,
guilty of laziness
           corruption
           intolerance
           absenteeism
           irresponsibility.

N.B. (i) Remember, both here and everywhere else in this book, generalisations are being made. All generalisations are to be treated warily.

For instance, the above remarks about the Church apply only to the higher echelons of that body. The majority of the lower orders (the village *curé*) were poor, hard-working priests, anxious for the welfare of their flock.

And that, in its turn, does not mean that there was no such thing as a conscientious bishop or a corrupt *curé*.

(ii) Students who approach the French Revolution for the first time, whose knowledge probably stems from Dickens or Baroness Orczy, tend to underestimate the part of the Church.

The French Revolution proved to be almost as much anti-Church as it did anti-nobility.

4. The bourgeoisie How far is it true to say that nearly every country which produces a challenge to its established government has a middle class which is 'rising'?

Remember the nobility were not allowed to engage in commerce, which, therefore, left a large field of opportunity open to others.

It is another fairly normal process in history that when a group or class gains economic power, its next step is to demand a share in political power. (Witness the English Industrial Revolution and the industrialists' entry into politics after 1832.)

And, incidentally, it was the middle class which produced many of the leaders of the Revolution—Desmoulins, Danton, Robespierre, for example.

5. The Peasantry   Who were owner-occupiers, by the way, of nearly 40 per cent of the land.

Their objections to feudal privileges of the nobility
government monopolies
unfair taxes
a lack of government generally.

It has been commented that the peasant,

if he owned his land (or at any rate had some owner's rights),
if he had the strength to revolt,
if he possessed the wealth actually to pay all these taxes,
could not have been 'crushed with tyranny'.

Perhaps 'exasperated' would be a more apt comment than 'oppressed'.

6. Government   Over-centralised.
The lack of uniformity. E.g. *Pays d'état* and *pays d'élection*.

Provincial traditions died hard, the relics of feudal separatism.

The hopeless complexity of internal customs barriers, and its consequent effect on trade.

Taxation —Irregular and out-of-date.
Unfairly and inconsistently assessed.
Corruption and embezzlement prevented much of it reaching Paris.

Attempts at reform by Turgot had been scotched by the nobility in the 1770s, but he had had time to give a glimpse of what was possible. That made reversion to the old ways after his fall all the more intolerable.

Louis XVI didn't help matters by his frequently-expressed desire to promote reforms—he talked and hoped, but he didn't *do* anything.

7. Ideas

The Encyclopaedists were extending the frontiers of men's minds and developing their powers of criticism.

Rousseau's *Du Contrat Social* became necessary reading for all aspiring revolutionaries.

Montesquieu's *L'Esprit des Lois*, more highbrow, but influential nevertheless among thinking men.

Voltaire, a figure of European renown, biting critic of the Church, champion of lost causes, a sort of private Ombudsman to Western Europe.

The Parlements of France, in their opposition to the Crown, produced arguments which were later used to develop the theory of constitutional rule, and of limitations on executive powers.

N.B. Ideas, by themselves, don't usually start revolutions. The Rousseaus and the Voltaires and the Diderots did not create the problems mentioned above, nor did they make them worse.

But they did bring them to the forefront of men's minds. They did help to start the train of thought which led from 'this is so' to 'this should not be so' to 'we can do something about it'.

8. The economy   Was the French economy in trouble?
There are as many sets of statistics as there are books, all to prove practically anything you like. Before using any of them, it is wise to check, to see

(a) to what period of time they refer.
(b) to what section of France they apply. (Normandy, for example, was a wealthier province than Brittany.)

What then, is there to go on?

(a) the very fact that there was a revolution would appear to indicate that there might have been something wrong.
(b) there is some evidence of a discrepancy between the rise in prices and the rise in wages during the eighteenth century.
(c) France lost three wars out of four with England between 1702 and 1783, handing over her empires in India and Canada, and sundry wealthy West Indian islands.

Against this must be set

(i) France's size (in comparison with other West European countries)

her compactness

her population (two to three times bigger than England's, for example)

her still formidable naval and commercial fleet.

(ii) the fact that the bourgeoisie, by and large, were, as stated above, 'rising'—so they must have been making money.

Every so often, in the writing of an answer, you may have to stop, because you can't think of what to say next—though you may be uncomfortably aware that there is plenty more that needs saying.

If you get stuck for ideas, either on what to say or on how to present it, it sometimes helps to take the question to pieces.

For example, a few ideas have been provided on 'why did a revolution break out'. Now consider the '1789' part of it. Why did the Revolution occur in 1789? Why not 1779 or 1799?

Again, these remarks do not so much 'tell you the answer' as suggest ideas which could usefully be examined, topics which might profitably be studied, lines of thought which might be worth following.

9. America 1775–1783	The shining example of liberty, achieved moreover by an army of 'citizens'.

Frenchmen had fought in that war. Lafayette was to become the darling of the Paris crowd.

Ideas incidentally went two ways: Montesquieu's writings were studied in the framing of the American Constitution.

10. Money, or rather the lack of it.

Ironically, despite her technical success in the American War, France's finances suffered a severe setback as a result of it. Remember too the accumulated financial strain of Louis XIV's extravagance, and Louis XV's wars.

A succession of finance ministers proved unable to cope.

It is surprising how many problems boil down to a plain, sordid lack of money.

11. The Notables 1787	As the name suggests, an assembly of notabilities, summoned to discuss the financial crisis.

Ministers and Notables alike had one remedy shrieking at them—abolition of tax exemption for clergy and nobility.

Few had the honesty to suggest it, and none, not even the King, could overcome the entrenched opposition of the privileged orders.

So in a sense it was not the lower orders who started the Revolution, nor the bourgeoisie, but the aristocracy.

> It was the aristocracy which (in practice if not in theory) began the opposition to the monarchy.
>
> It was the intransigence of the Notables in refusing to accept the principle of universal taxation, and their passing of the buck to the States-General, which led to the gathering of the first national representative body in France for 175 years and so provided the vehicle for expression of grievances.

12. The Dutch Crisis   A serious diplomatic defeat for France, which
    1787–88   discredited the Government accordingly.

Feeble or unsuccessful conduct of foreign affairs is rarely, if ever, the deciding factor in the fall of a regime, but it is quite a common contributory one:

> E.g. Charles I (Stuart) and his unsuccessful campaigns in France, Spain, and Scotland.
>
> Louis-Philippe and his unpopular record of 'servility' to England.
>
> Tsar Nicholas II and his failures against Japan and Germany.

13. The Eden Treaty   England made much more profit out of it than
    1786   France. Many English goods drove their French counterparts off the market.

> Governments tend to get blamed for slumps and fluctuating prices and unemployment, even in the eighteenth century, when they had far less control over them.

(Incidentally, why would it be, in a sense, more logical to mention the Eden Treaty of 1786 like this, *after* the Dutch Crisis of 1787, than before?)

14. The weather | The winter of 1788–89 was the hardest for eighty years.

Bad summer weather usually means a bad harvest, which means in turn high bread prices. And there is often a close tally between high bread prices and revolutionary agitation:

> E.g. In France 1789–95 | The number of disturbances that took place around July and August, before the harvest came through.

> In England 1820s to 1840s | Note how often a bad harvest coincided with agricultural revolts or strikes or petitions for reform.

15. June and July, 1789 | The Tennis Court Oath.

The 'Great Fear'.

The presence of Broglie's army near Paris.

The dismissal of Necker.

The fact that the Bastille was said to be an arsenal as well as a prison.

To be really thorough, you should deal also with the 'in France' phrase of the question as well.

Why did a revolution break out in France, rather than anywhere else?

But to do justice to that would require a full comparative study of the economy, politics and society of the other powers in Europe, for which there is not sufficient time in any essay of this scope.

And anyway, there were revolutionary disturbances in other places round about 1789:

E.g. 1780 The Gordon Riots had terrorised London for four days.

1783 European ministers at Versailles officially condoned the rebellion of George III's subjects in America.

1787 The rising of the 'Patriots' against the Stadtholder in Holland.

1790 The year of Emperor Joseph's death saw risings among his Belgian and Magyar subjects.

1795 The last gallant attempt to reassert Polish independence.

Even so, it is generally agreed that there was something special about the French Revolution, and one or two random comments of a general nature would provide you with a means of ending the essay. Finishing essays can be almost as difficult as starting them.

16. Was it because France was not worse off but *better* off than other countries?

How did her general standards of education compare with those of the rest of Europe?

Her peasants, one is led to believe, could actually afford to pay all these taxes.

Her middle classes were doing well.

Turgot in the 1770s had given a glimpse of Elysium.

Paris was the cultural centre of Europe.

The starving and downtrodden rarely have the energy to revolt, but the vigorous and the well-to-do might seek to better themselves.

17. Was it the rigidity of class divisions in France?

There was class distinction in England, but an able man, a rich man, or a lucky man could enter the ranks of upper society. How many of Napoleon's marshals, for instance, would have reached commissioned rank in the army of Louis XVI?

18. Was it that French feudalism, despite its social irritants, was in fact economically weaker than its counterparts in Central Europe?

Serfdom, for instance, survived in Hungary till 1848,
in Russia till 1861.

Even within France, the *La Vendée* district, where feudalism was strongest, boasted the strongest Royalist tradition.

Reading list

A. COBBAN, *A History of Modern France*, Vol. I, Pelican, 1965.
A. GOODWIN, *The French Revolution*, Hutchinson, 1966.
H. KURTZ, *The Emigrés*, History Today, February, 1963.
G. LEFÈBVRE, *The French Revolution, 1789–93*, Routledge, 1962.
G. RUDÉ, *The Crowd in the French Revolution*, Oxford, 1959.
G. RUDÉ, *The Fall of the Bastille*, History Today, July, 1954.
G. SALVEMINI, *The French Revolution, 1788–92*, Cape, 1954.
J. H. SHENNAN, *The Parlement of Paris*, History Today, May, 1960.
J. M. THOMPSON, *The French Revolution*, Blackwell, 1943.
A. DE TOCQUEVILLE, *The Ancien Régime and the French Revolution*, Blackwell, 1947; Fontana, 1966.
E. L. WOODWARD, *French Revolutions*, Oxford, 1934.

2 'The great tragedy of the French Revolution was the War.' Discuss

This essay is difficult—inasmuch as you have to look at the French Revolution as a whole.

It is also easy—you are simply being asked your opinion. In a sense it doesn't matter, within reason, what you say, as long as you back it up with a fair amount of fact and some degree of logic.

You will have realised by now that more time and attention is focused on the French Revolution than on almost any other topic in modern history. (This is not the time to enter into a discussion as to why this should be.) One of the results of this tends to be an inordinately large pile of 'A' Level notes on every twist and turn the Revolution takes from 1789 onwards, almost month by month. The problem becomes one not of lack of material, but of surfeit. This is complicated further when the question involves not one feature of the Revolution, but the whole of it.

It therefore becomes doubly important that you 'think big'. You must get far enough back to enable you to see the salient features. And you will not be able to do this if uppermost in your mind is the urgent desire to get on paper the large number of detailed facts you have laboriously collected. If you cannot make your favourite facts like

Danton was born at Arcis-sur-Aube.

Louis XVI was executed on the feast of St. Agnes.

The Revolutionary Tribunal in Paris condemned to death 2,639 people.

belong to any part of your argument, then you must deny yourself the luxury of using them. The bigger the scope of the essay, the more important it becomes to have arguments first, facts second.

So, to repeat—THINK BIG.

And, while you're about it—THINK SIMPLE.

What in effect, are you going to say in this essay?

1. The war *was* the great tragedy—finish.

2. The war was a tragedy, but only up to a point.

3. Other things were much more tragic than the war.

4. The war was a mixed blessing.

5. The war, far from being a tragedy, was the best thing that could have happened to the Revolution.

6. The French Revolution didn't 'have' a tragedy at all.

Don't worry unduly about being absolutely right; there are very few if any right answers in history. Just examine the evidence, draw your own conclusions, make up your mind what you're going to say, and say it.

Get your terms of reference clear too. In this case, the operative phrase is 'French Revolution'. How big a period of time do you consider this covers? When does the Revolution 'end'? Arguably

August 10th, 1792.

January 21st, 1793.

Thermidor, the fall of Robespierre.

Vendémiaire, the dying gasp of the people of Paris.

Brumaire, Bonaparte's coup.

Amiens, the truce between France and Europe, when the Powers admitted their inability to crush the Revolution.

Napoleon's Imperial Coronation.

For that matter, when does the French Revolution 'begin'?

The aristocratic revolt of 1787–88.

The decision to summon the States-General.

The Tennis Court Oath.

The *Séance Royale*.

The storming of the Bastille.

The great surrender of feudal privileges on August 4th.

The Declaration of the Rights of Man.

The removing of the Royal Family and the National Assembly from Versailles to Paris, closer to the mob.

What follows is little more than a collection of suggestions. You will probably accept some of them; it is extremely unlikely that you will accept them all. But when you disagree, ask yourself why. These reasons will help you to build your own verdict—which is the object of the exercise.

What did the war do to upset the Revolution?

(i) It divided the Legislative Assembly, already short on political experience as a result of the Self-Denying Ordinance passed by the Constituent Assembly.

(ii) The early French defeats, and Brunswick's Manifesto, led to the risings of August 10th, the setting up of a republic, and the September Massacres.

(iii) The necessity for strong central authority to run the war produced

committee government.

re-centralisation far more stringent than the old Bourbon system pulled down with the Bastille.

spies, informers, secret police, summary 'justice', an overworked guillotine.

all the machinery of the Terror, in contradiction of the original ideals and aspirations of the early revolutionaries

liberty and equality.

freedom of speech.

giving initiative to local authorities.

the right to a fair trial, and so on.

(iv) Defeats in 1793 led to the removal of the Girondins, and laid the way open for Jacobin extremists.

(v) Preoccupation with the war prevented the government from dealing properly with the teething troubles resulting from the original reforms, while the war itself made these problems infinitely worse.

E.g. Local government

The judicial reforms

The Civil Constitution of the Clergy

The control of royalism

Taxation

Assignats and the sale of Church land.

(vi) Defeats, especially at the hands of the British, led to

loss of vital colonies.

the virtual destruction and/or immobilisation of the navy.

the near strangulation of trade due to the naval blockade.

These were all serious blows to a country struggling to put its new house in order.

(vii) The war, by making unified command, and force, necessary, resulted in

the Directory's reliance on the army to annul the verdict of unwelcome elections.

the emergence of Bonaparte as head of state.

in complete denial of the revolution's original aim to curb the power of an over-mighty, arbitrary central authority.

On the other hand, the war was responsible for

pulling together scattered minorities for the defence of France.

the *levée en masse* and the 'career of the talents', which produced a blazing outburst of military talent and organising genius to dazzle Europe.

taking France to a pinnacle of prestige and power she has not approached since.

producing in Napoleon a ruler of demonic energy who carried out reforms of staggering thoroughness and surprising permanence in nearly every branch of government.

spreading the ideas of 'revolution' all over Europe far more effectively than a million pamphlets could have done.

What about the other possible 'tragedies' of the Revolution? The following are offered with no implied order of importance or validity.

(i) Louis XVI

Note the parallels with Charles I of England and Nicholas II of Russia. Was it a tragedy that these three men, sincere in their own way, failed to provide inspiration and leadership at the very time that their struggling peoples needed it?

Or was it rather their weaknesses of character which caused their respective revolutions to occur when they did?

(ii) The death of Mirabeau, the one great personality of the early days. With his aristocratic birth and radical politics, he might have been able to pull the dissident groups in society together—reminiscent of Cicero's dream of a *concordia ordinum*.

(iii) The loss of control by the bourgeois, the middle-class moderates. They wanted the impossible—a half-way revolution. They were not prepared to follow their ideas and premises to their logical conclusions, unlike the doctrinaire Robespierre.

And when the middle-class regained a measure of control in 1795, they soon lost it again, this time to the Right, not to the Left.

(iv) Paris and its mob.

Had the Royal Family been left in Versailles (or had they even been allowed to escape, as James II was), and had the Assemblies not been so vulnerable to mob activity, perhaps the Revolution would have enjoyed a smoother career.

(v) The quarrel with the Papacy, symbolised in the Civil Constitution of the Clergy.

Did this really split French society from top to bottom and so alienate a lot of potential allegiance to the Revolution, or did it merely bring to the surface a vein of anti-clericalism long embedded in the French character?

(vi) The French psychological weakness for strong government, ingrained into them by the tradition of Richelieu and Louis XIV.

1789 produced Bonaparte
1848 produced Louis-Napoleon
1958 produced de Gaulle

Is it fair to read any kind of pattern into this?

(vii) The mere fact that it was a revolution in the mechanical sense of the word, a full circle.

Is it tragic, ironic, inevitable (or all three) that popular movements against autocratic rule so often end up where they started?

E.g. Charles I — Cromwell
Louis XVI — Napoleon
Nicholas II — Lenin
Alfonso — Franco
Farouk — Nasser
Battista — Castro

Is the only 'un-tragic' revolution the one that can stop half-way, like, say, the one which created the U.S.A.?

Reading list

A. COBBAN, *A History of Modern France*, Vol. I. Pelican, 1965.
A. GOODWIN, *The French Revolution*, Hutchinson, 1966.
G. LEFÈBVRE, *The French Revolution, 1789–93*, Routledge, 1962.
G. LEFÈBVRE, *The Thermidoreans*, Routledge, 1965.
R. R. PALMER, *Twelve Who Ruled*, Princeton, 1941.
G. RUDÉ, *The Crowd in the French Revolution*, Oxford, 1959.
M. J. SYDENHAM, *The Girondins*, Athlone, 1961.
J. M. THOMPSON, *The French Revolution*, Blackwell, 1943.
J. M. THOMPSON, *Leaders of the French Revolution*, Blackwell, 1928.
E. L. WOODWARD, *French Revolutions*, Oxford, 1934.

3   How and why did Bonaparte come to power?

Nearly every examination paper contains at least one biographical essay. Such essays are attractive inasmuch as one has no trouble about a central theme, a spine for the argument. But—and here's the snag—they are usually so worded that you should not write a brief biography by way of answer. As a rule it is only in 'O' Level that you get asked questions like 'Write an account of the career of Napoleon'.

The requirements now are rather more subtle. You should select whatever biographical detail you need, and present it in such a way that it fits into the overall argument you are constructing.

(i)   Try and get away from bare statements of fact like 'Napoleone Buonaparte was the second son born to a petty Corsican nobleman in August 1769, and he became a military cadet when he was only nine', in which you carefully use the Italian spelling of his name to show how accurate and knowledgeable you are.

A deeper analysis of the facts, and a different presentation of them, ought to produce something more incisive, along the lines of: 'The annexation of Corsica by France in 1768 came just in time for Napoleon to be born French, and to benefit from the new military reforms whereby sons of poor nobles could be educated in French academies at royal expense. Because Carlo Bonaparte decided that his eldest son, Joseph, would never make a soldier, it was the second son, Napoleon, who received the opportunity to join the mainstream of eighteenth-century life and thought.'

In each case you are concerned with the date of his birth, his position in the family, and his social and national origins.

(ii)   Take the Italian Campaign of 1796–97. If you said, 'Bonaparte was given the Italian Command, beat the Sardinians at Mondovi, and the Austrians at Lodi, Castiglione, Arcola, and Rivoli, and signed preliminaries of peace at Leoben,' you would be stating incontrovertible fact.

But from the point of view of the essay, would it not have been better to draw attention to the following:

28

It was the sheer number, swiftness, and completeness of the victories which stupefied friend and foe alike, and marked him as something special.

By turning what was originally a sideshow into the main campaign and knocking out the chief enemy in Europe, he became the hero of France.

By judicious looting and timely extortion, he became the first revolutionary general to make war pay.

By taking it upon himself to engage in political negotiations at Leoben, he began to expose the vulnerability of the Directors.

By all means mention names, dates, facts and figures, but always keep them subservient to the argument.

Bonaparte's early years, and his handling of the Italian Campaign, clearly have some bearing on his rise to power. It is for you to decide what that bearing is before you talk about these two factors.

The same applies to the other stages in his career. Always arrange the facts so that they point in the direction of the argument.

Now that they've been mentioned, what are these other stages in his rise to power which deserve attention?

What is the relevance (if any) of

his military education at Brienne and Paris.
his early postings at Valence and Auxonne.
his clashes with the Paolists in Corsica.
his stay in Paris in 1792.
the Toulon episode, 1793.
his command in the Army of the South.
the rising of *Vendémiaire*, 1795.
Italy (as suggested above).
the *coup d'état* of *Fructidor*, 1797.
the Egyptian Campaign, 1798.
the negotiations with Sieyès, Talleyrand, and Fouché, 1799.
the *coup d'état* of *Brumaire*, 1799.
the new consular constitution.

Collect the necessary information, and see how many of the facts can be arranged to point in the direction of the argument.

Of course, there's a bit more to it than that. Bonaparte wasn't tall, smart, imposing, rich, or influential. But he must have had *something*.

(i) Personal qualities

Did his Corsican insularity and consequent loneliness produce the necessary drive and ambition?

Is there anything in the fact that, like Churchill, Lenin, and Hitler in their formative, pre-celebrity days, Napoleon as a youth went through a phase of being a voracious reader.

Did he possess blazing intelligence, or merely a gargantuan capacity for work, or both?

Was he a ruthless careerist, or a gifted opportunist?

Did his Corsican origins give him a sense of callous detachment in his attitude to French politics, a sense denied to his rivals?

Genius is an elusive quality to pin down. What is it? And did Bonaparte possess it?

(ii) Luck

Many authorities from Julius Caesar to Winston Churchill (including Bonaparte himself) have declared luck to be an indispensable ingredient of success. Others would have us believe that, with a combination of skill, application, determination, and optimism, a man makes his own luck.
So take your pick.

Would it have made any difference if Bonaparte had been commissioned into the Navy and not the Army? (Because he nearly was.)

Was it really luck that decreed he should be in Paris in 1795 at the very time the Convention wanted a military commander to quell the royalist rising?

Did the stars in their courses fight against Nelson in his frantic dashes across the Mediterranean looking for the Egyptian expedition?

(iii) Timely assistance
Where and when was Bonaparte given necessary help? What did he owe (if anything) to

Saliceti
Augustin Robespierre
Barras
Augereau
Sieyès
his brother Lucien.

And what about his mistakes? He made them, the same as anybody else.

E.g. How did he survive his defeats in Corsica at the hands of the Paolists?

How did he escape retribution in 1794 during the witch-hunts for members of the Robespierrist faction?

Look what happened to the Egyptian expedition. How was he able to ride that storm?

His marriage to Josephine may have staggered Parisian society, but did it further his career?

He didn't run a particularly efficient *coup d'état* in 1799. What saw him through?

Remember, however gifted or lucky the man, the times in which he lived always offer some clue to his success. Just how far these times account for a man's success is one of the endless debates of history.

What is the ultimate determining factor—human personality or impersonal forces and trends? Decide for yourself.

But you need to be aware, and to make it clear that you are aware, of the two elements.

So consider the broader aspects of the problem.

(i) The Directory

How well was it running the war?
How healthy (or unhealthy) was France's internal economy?
How fairly did it represent public opinion in France?

E.g.   Royalists
       Jacobins
       Thermidoreans

How valuable as a precedent was the Directors' reliance on military force in *Vendémiaire*, 1795, and *Fructidor*, 1797?

What was the effect on their reputation and power of the various coups in 1797, 1798, and 1799 to annul the results of unfavourable elections?

(ii) The War

> Could five Directors run a coherent war policy (provided one of them was Carnot), or was there really a need for a single Commander-in-Chief?
>
> To what extent did Frenchmen become bewitched by *La Gloire* following Bonaparte's early victories? And incidentally how big a part was played by Bonaparte's own propaganda machine?
>
> Was Bonaparte really the saviour of France in 1799? Hadn't Masséna, by his defeat of Suvorov, already saved it? If so, what was Bonaparte saving France from? (There are some careful distinctions to be made between what Frenchmen *thought* was happening, and what actually *was* happening.)
>
> The war threw up a host of highly competent commanders in the late 1790s   Hoche
>   Jourdan
>   Pichegru
>   Moreau
>   Bernadotte,
>   and others.
>
> Why did Sieyès choose Bonaparte, and not one of them? Wasn't this coup a practical proposition for any successful general?

(iii) The Revolution

> Did Bonaparte owe anything to the great social changes brought about since 1789?
>
> What would be the average Frenchman's attitude to the remorseless succession of assemblies, and elections, and coups, and constitutions?

(iv) What were Frenchmen afraid of?

> The enemy?
> After the campaigns of Bonaparte himself, of Moreau, and Masséna, how serious a threat was the Second Coalition?
>
> The Royalists?
> Similarly, how likely was the prospect of a White Terror?
>
> A return of Popery?

A re-distribution of their newly-won Church lands?

Loss of the franchise?
How interested were they in elections now?

What did Bonaparte have to offer to allay these fears?

Finally, there happens to be a tailor-made quotation from a contemporary authority which fits the situation, and which serves well as
either introduction or conclusion.

Look up Edmund Burke's comments on the 'popular general' in
his *Reflections on the Revolution in France.* See if you agree with
his argument.

Reading list

C. BRINTON, *A Decade of Revolution*, Harper & Row, 1934.
D. G. CHANDLER, *The Campaigns of Napoleon*, Weidenfeld &
Nicolson, 1967.
A. COBBAN, *A History of Modern France*, Vol. I. Pelican, 1965.
H. A. L. FISHER, *Napoleon*, Oxford, 1967.
G. LEFÈBVRE, *The Directory*, Routledge, 1965.
G. LEFÈBVRE, *Napoleon*, Routledge, 1969.
E. LUDWIG, *Napoleon*, Allen & Unwin, 1927.
F. M. H. MARKHAM, *Napoleon and the Awakening of Europe*, E.U.P.,
1954.
J. M. THOMPSON, *Napoleon Bonaparte: His Rise and Fall*, Blackwell,
1951.
J. M. THOMPSON (Ed.), *Napoleon's Letters*, Everyman Edition.

4 Compare the parts played by Spain and Russia in the downfall of Napoleon

Here is a good example of the pitfall question. It is temptingly easy to write a great deal on 'Spain and Russia against Napoleon', without saying very much about the question.

For example

(i) While details of marches, sieges, and battles in the Pensinsular War often escape the memory, the reasons for Allied success (or, if you like, French failure) have an odd trick of sticking.

Now it is a very human weakness, if one has at one's disposal a well-organised set of facts, to want to use them in an examination. The candidate, his head bursting with information about the lines of Torres Vedras, and Napoleon's out-of-date orders, and the quarrels between his Marshals, and British command of the sea, and so on, sees the words 'Spain' and 'downfall of Napoleon'. Because he happens to have learnt the reasons for the downfall of Napoleon in Spain, he is often misled into thinking that that is what the question is asking him to explain.

(ii) Certain events in history catch the imagination. Napoleon's Retreat from Moscow is one of them. Whatever the reason—the dramatic unity of the whole thing, the titanic scale of it, the theme of the humbling of the mighty, the helplessness of man against the elements, the melodramatic value of fur-capped Cossacks galloping out of the snowy darkness, and so on—people enjoy reading about it, and remember it easily. And if a candidate has prepared this exciting section of Russian history as an examination topic, it is a logical next step to want to write about it.

So a teacher feels bound to offer the somewhat depressing piece of advice that the candidate should not enjoy his work too much—at least not to the extent of pursuing study of the exciting episodes to the exclusion of the more sober, scholarly side.

Examiners, unfortunately, require you to supply information
and comment on topics of *their* choosing: they do not, alas!
ask you to tell them all about what you are interested in.
(Which is, some say, a pity; they might get much less boring
stuff to read.)

The fact still remains though, that in order to answer the
question one must discuss the war in Spain and the Retreat
from Moscow.

However, there is more than one way of talking about the Peninsular War and the Russian Campaign.

As briefly as possible, you are being asked not what Napoleon
did *in* Spain and Russia, but what the two countries did *to* Napoleon.

A convenient starting-point is the similarity in the pattern of relations between France and Spain and between France and Russia.
In both cases a period of initial hostility was followed by one of
alliance, which, becoming more and more strained, broke under the
pressure of Napoleonic bullying and led finally to permanent, and
extremely bitter conflict:

1. Spain
The First Coalition.
The Treaty of San Ildefonso.
Brother Joseph dumped on the throne.
Military occupation and government.
The War of Independence.

2. Russia
The Second Coalition.
The Armed Neutrality.
The Third Coalition.
The Treaty of Tilsit.
The quarrels over the Continental blockade.
The campaign of 1812.
The Fourth Coalition.

Another one is Napoleon's own oft-quoted comment about the
'Spanish ulcer', the idea being that because the verdict is personal and
contemporary, therefore it must be authoritative and accurate.
Clearly such comments are valuable, but they are not infallible, so
don't forget to consider the 'ulcer' remark in the light of the facts.
And remember too that Napoleon was so impulsive and energetic
that he passed remarks about almost everything.

It might be worth setting against the 'ulcer' cliché the exasperated
outburst of Wellington, after his Spanish regulars had run away
(again) at Talavera: 'I have never known the Spaniards do *anything*,
much less do anything well.'

Are the two opinions reconcilable?

The remarks that follow are little more than suggestions. The merit of your answer depends on the skill with which you fashion your facts into a coherent argument.

1. Spain's contribution.

  (i) The surrender of the French at Bailen

      The first serious setback to French armies since 1798 (ironically, against the great Russian general, Suvorov).

      The news echoed round Europe.

      BUT—did it stimulate the *Spanish* army to further military triumphs?

  (ii) Spain was the stronghold of Catholic conservatism. How far did Spanish resistance represent and encourage Church traditionalism against the, then, modern trend of cynical conformity engineered by Bonaparte, especially after his shabby treatment of the Pope?

  (iii) How much of the credit for Spain's contribution really belongs to Wellington and his Peninsular Army? What did the Duke mean when he referred to his troops as 'the scum of the earth'?

      Was it rather that Spain was important only inasmuch as it provided a training-ground for the army and the commander that ultimately was to beat the master at his own game? (An interesting parallel, here, with Scipio and Hannibal.)

  (iv) What really caught Europe's imagination?

      The set-piece battles?
      The bitter sieges like Saragossa and Gerona?
      The (exaggerated?) stories of atrocities and reprisals?

  (v) Did Spanish resistance *really, consciously*, encourage others?

      Did it inspire the great architects of Prussia's revival?

      Did it induce the Austrians to try yet again in 1809 and 1813?

      Was it a popular war in England?

      Did the Russians fight so bitterly in 1812 because of the inspiration of Spain?

(vi) What did Spain do to the French army?

    Destroy it?

    Defeat it?

    Keep it occupied?

    Sap its morale?

    Ruin its marshals' reputations?
    (Oddly enough, Marshal Ney, dismissed from his Corps Command in Spain, re-emerged a year later as the hero of the Russian Retreat.)

(vii) How could a country like Spain be a force in Europe when there were so many factions and disagreements within it?

    Liberals v Monarchists.

    Loyalists v collaborators (the *afrancesados*).

    The generals v the civil juntas.

    The traditionalist peasants v the sophisticated town 'progressives'.

    The regular army v the guerrillas.

(viii) Was it simply that the Spanish War of Independence dragged on, and on, and on?

2. Russia's contribution.

    (i) Like Everest, simply being 'there'. Could a military tyrant like Bonaparte really tolerate the presence in 'his' continent of one great power still un-awed? Was it this which tempted him to his classic folly?

    (ii) Obviously 1812 itself.

        Clearly the Napoleonic machine was not invincible.

        Equally clearly the moral effect on both sides was tremendous.

Many historians would have it that Napoleon himself went into a decline afterwards. A moral one, a psychological one, or a physiological one? (Depends on which historian you read.) And anyway, does *post quod* mean *propter quod*?

The actual losses in manpower. Again, statistics vary (see *History Today*, April 1960), but they were all huge by contemporary standards. What is the effect of this on Bonaparte's campaigns in 1813 and 1814?

The much discussed Russian winter. How many casualties were the result of the cold (i.e. attributable to Russia) and how many were the result of hunger, disease and over-stretched lines of communication (i.e. attributable to French miscalculation).

What connection is there between 1812 and the Fourth Coalition and Wars of Liberation?

(iii) How many Russian troops were employed in the campaigns of 1813 and 1814, and were ready to be employed in 1815?

(iv) What was the nature of the Russian military contribution?

The bovine stolidity of the peasant soldier?

The generalship of Barclay and Kutuzov?

The pulverising power of Russian artillery, for instance at Eylau, Borodino or the Beresina? (Ironic that Bonaparte was a gunner by training.)

Sheer numbers? Every European commander from Frederick the Great onwards found that the Russians just kept on coming. (Again ironic for the country which produced the *levée en masse*.)

And incidentally, what was the Russian Navy doing all this time?

(v) What was Russia's diplomatic role in the alliance against Bonaparte?
How reliable was she as a member of coalitions?

How useful or valid are comments like—

The Russian campaign lasted for less than one year, but the Spanish one dragged on for six.

Spain only defeated the Marshals; Russia defeated Napoleon.

Spain needed Wellington and the British; Russia did it alone.

Have the two 'contributions' anything in common?

Economic.
Both wars were the result of Napoleon's attempts to seal off Europe from Britain.
Both countries were open ends of his unsuccessful Continental blockade.

Political.
Much is talked of 'nationalism' in this context. Again it is odd (or maybe fitting) that the great force harnessed by Bonaparte— aggressive French nationalism—should be checked by its defensive counterpart in Spain and Russia. Perhaps it was the one force that could check it.

Geographical.
The saying about 'where small armies are defeated and large armies starve' could be applied with some truth to both. Spain and Russia represented forces which no man could master. (Who knows? If Bonaparte had ever invaded England, perhaps the weather would have driven him home again!)

Psychological.
Is there anything in the idea that Bonaparte, the great moderniser, the classic amoral genius, was defeated by backward pauperised partisans and peasant soldiers who owed unhesitating allegiance to national autocrats and conservative churches? Was it that Spain and Russia somehow represented some permanent values in the world of constant violence and flux perpetuated by Bonaparte?

In the last resort, does their contribution become effective by virtue of the fact that, for two or three years, they were both happening *at the same time*?

N.B. Comparisons and Estimates.

The question said 'compare', which is what you must obviously do.
Sometimes, however, the examiners say not 'compare' but
'estimate'. The same material is applicable, of course, but the word
'estimate' usually implies something else—a setting of your valua-
tion in its overall context. In this case the overall context is the defeat
of Napoleon. So having stated your case, you should make a *passing
reference* to things like British obstinacy, the loss of command of the
sea by Bonaparte, the gradual exhaustion of France, the revival of
Prussia, and so on—to let the examiner see that you are aware of the
scope of the overall picture.

Reading list

F. ALTAMIRA, *A History of Spain*, Van Norstrand, 1949.

W. C. ATKINSON, *A History of Spain and Portugal*, Pelican, 1967.

A. BRYANT, *The Years of Victory*, Collins, 1944.

A. BRYANT, *The Age of Elegance*, Collins, 1954.

R. CARR, *Spain, 1808–1939*, Oxford, 1966.

D. G. CHANDLER, *The Campaigns of Napoleon*, Weidenfeld &
Nicolson, 1967.

R. F. DELDERFIELD, *The Retreat from Moscow*, Hodder, 1967.

L. KOCHAN, *The Making of Modern Russia*, Pelican, 1963.

A. G. MACDONNELL, *Napoleon and his Marshals*, Macmillan, 1934.

B. PARES, *A History of Russia*, Cape, 1955.

N. V. RIASONOVSKY, *A History of Russia*, Oxford, 1963.

G. RUDÉ, *Revolutionary Europe*, Fontana, 1964.

D. STURLEY, *A Short History of Modern Russia*, Longmans, 1964.

E. TARLÉ, *The Russian Campaign of 1812*, Allen & Unwin, 1942.

J. M. THOMPSON, *Napoleon Bonaparte: His Rise and Fall*, Blackwell,
1951.

J. WELLER, *Wellington in the Peninsula*, Vane, 1962.

5 Why did the Fourth Coalition succeed where the others failed?

Possibly the easiest question on any paper covering this period—certainly one of the easiest. Occasionally the examiners practically spell it out for you by saying something like: 'Account for the final collapse of France in 1814.' They are more likely, however, to try and wrap it up a bit, so you might see instead things like:

- (i) 'From 1810 onwards the Napoleonic Empire was in decline.' Discuss.
- (ii) How far was Napoleon's overthrow due to his underrating of national feeling in Europe?
- (iii) 'The decisive factor in Napoleon's downfall was his decision to invade Russia.' Discuss.
- (iv) Any one of several quotations made by the Emperor himself about what betrayed him—which again you are invited to discuss.

But in each case you are being given the chance to display your knowledge of the various factors relating to the defeat of France. Clearly you wouldn't write the same essay for each question, but you would draw on the same material. It is a matter of presentation.

In (i) You would analyse the symptoms of decline after 1810, and find quite probably that some of the causes go back before 1810. Alternatively you might find that the causes of decline do not become operative until after 1810.
   (ii) Calls for the setting of nationalism's strength and importance against that of all the other factors influencing Napoleon's overthrow.
   (iii) Demands a similar assessment. Was the 'decision to invade Russia' the really decisive factor (and, if so, how), or was it another factor, or a group of factors, which tipped the scale (and, if so, how)? Remember here you are being asked to find not the biggest factor, but the decisive one—which is not necessarily the same.

(iv) Is similar to (iii). Was it really 'the Spanish ulcer' or 'Marshal Marmont' which betrayed him? If so, in what way? If not, what was it? And how? (And of course you might query the word 'betrayed'.)

In all four, and in the original 'Fourth Coalition' question, you are being required to argue about the collapse of the Napoleonic Empire. And things like the Fourth Coalition, 1810, national feeling, the invasion of Russia, the Spanish Ulcer, and Marshal Marmont, are merely hooks on which to hang the argument.

Just how much of the essay you devote to explaining why the first three coalitions failed is a debatable point, but you ought to devote a little at any rate, if only because

(i) It would serve as a perfectly adequate introduction.
(ii) It would provide the clues for the rest of the essay. Many of the reasons for failure in the First, Second, and Third Coalitions, *in reverse*, will be reasons for the Fourth Coalition's success.

All this may sound very elementary, childishly simple, almost obvious. But you cannot afford to miss the obvious; you must be able to see the problem in its simple outline before you wade into the detail; and Mr. Holmes always said his most brilliant deductions were 'elementary'.

So, why did the first three coalitions fail?
Think in general terms for a moment. Why do coalitions fail?

(i) The most obvious—they're not good enough. So look for evidence of

poor commanders

inadequate armies   training
                             skill
                             weapons
                             mobility, etc.

uninspiring government leadership
                                      unmilitary kings
                                      Cabinet quarrels
                                      bumbling ministers

plain inefficiency
                             a poor supply system
                             bad communications
                             insufficient financial backing, and so on.

(ii) Almost equally obvious perhaps—the mere fact that they *are* coalitions. It takes an exterior threat of truly enormous proportions to produce a workable military partnership between sovereign states that will last for any length of time. After all, Hitler's Germany can reasonably be called a 'big threat' to rational civilisation. Yet even then, the bickering between the Allies (read something like the Alanbrooke Diaries) bedevilled every international conference, and made the creation of a universally acceptable strategy a task of terrifying hardship and complexity. How much more then, would allies be likely to quarrel in the 1790s, when France was taken nowhere near as seriously as Hitler's Germany in the 1940s.

(iii) Sheer numbers—not so much of population but of fighting men in the right place at the right time. It is usually when wars have been going on a long time that sheer population begins to count—when it becomes increasingly difficult to make good the losses.

(iv) The psychological factor—call it the 'will to win' if you like. Not *necessarily* vital (for example, it didn't bring success for Kosciuszko or Hofer or Kossuth), but, other things being equal, it can be important, even decisive.

You can probably think of other common reasons for the failure of coalitions. Having completed your list, apply it to the period 1793–1810; it should provide a lot of clues.

When you come to analysing the Fourth Coalition's success, the above factors *in reverse* may well apply.

Now comes the problem of arrangement of material. Once again, don't be afraid to be simple-minded. For instance, a perfectly feasible method is to arrange your points under the two headings

what the Fourth Coalition did right.
what the French did wrong.

You wouldn't use those phrases in an essay, naturally, but the somewhat crude division does provide a means of disciplining the facts, and allows you to 'see' the whole question.

What went right for the Coalition?

(i) Success
This is not saying that the Coalition won because it won; it is suggesting that because the Coalition took shape during a bad time for Napoleon, it at least got off to a good start. After his retreat from Russia, the Emperor's image (to use a modern term) was seriously impaired.

(ii) Sheer humdrum administrative efficiency.

For example

What did the British Army owe to Moore's new training schemes?

How did the reforms of Stein and Scharnhorst help Prussia to take an active part?

Were there any comparable improvements in Austria or Russia?

(iii) Learning from previous mistakes.

There is the story of the two French generals who had defected to the Allied side. They offered the unpalatable but practical advice that wherever the Allied troops met one of Napoleon's Marshals, they should attack; wherever they encountered the Emperor himself, they should retire. How far was this advice taken, and with what success?

How valuable was the experience that Wellington had gained in the Peninsular War?

(iv) Since Wellington has been mentioned, what was his contribution to Allied success? And that of Barclay de Tolly? And Kutuzov? And Blücher?

(v) What role did the diplomats play—Castlereagh, Metternich, for example?

(vi) Numbers, manpower, population.
Look up the figures for the Allied armies between 1812 and 1815.

(vii) Unity of purpose.

How and why were the members of the Fourth Coalition able to work together more effectively than their counterparts in the other three?

(viii) Economic strength.

Was the Fourth Coalition economically stronger than France?

Just how true was the legend of 'Pitt's gold'? Did Britain continue to subsidise the coalitions after Pitt's death?

What use was Britain's naval, commercial, and colonial strength?

(ix) The defections.

For example, Sweden and Bavaria changed sides.
Are these causes of Allied success, or symptoms?

N.B. Incidentally, it wasn't all success for the Allies, not by a long chalk. Examine the happenings at Lützen, Bautzen, Dresden, and Leipzig; Ligny and Quatre-Bras. Even Waterloo itself was 'a near-run thing'.

What went wrong for France?

(i) The changed role of France in Europe, from the liberator in the 1790s to the oppressor in the 1800s. Few people were taken in any more by French propaganda. Napoleon was seen not as a unique saviour or prophet, but as a French opportunist, typical of the tradition of Philip the Fair, Charles VIII, Richelieu, and Louis XIV; or, if you like, as a plain conqueror in the mould of Attila or Genghiz Khan.

(ii) Consider the effect of twenty years' almost non-stop war on a country virtually without allies, and moreover

ruled by a despot, who could no longer make war pay.

hounded by censorship and secret police.

torn by conscience over the treatment of the Pope.

stripped of colonial possessions.

drained of young men to fill the increasing gaps in the military ranks. (Look up the casualty figures for 1812–1814.)

forced to fight in 1814 on its own territory.

(iii) The Continental System.

What went wrong, and how did it backfire on its instigator?

(iv) Napoleon himself.

How far was he in decline after, say, 1812?

How far is his downfall due to his military mistakes and political errors of judgment?

Now try and develop some general idea, which sums up what you have been saying. Or make a stray comment which in your opinion points towards the decisive factor. But try and say something to finish the essay. Never let it end 'in the air'.

For instance

(i) Even if he'd won the Battle of Waterloo, Napoleon couldn't have gone on, because—and quote the figures for the Allied armies.

(ii) *In the end*, the Allies' will to win was greater than that of the French. Try and find a detailed instance which illustrates this. (You do not always have to conclude an essay with broad generalities.)

(iii) Time was on the Allies' side. The Napoleonic Empire was an artificial overgrowth, and in the nature of things could not survive. Did the Balance of Power in fact operate in politics like Newton's laws in physics?

(iv) It was all or nothing for Napoleon—world dominion or utter defeat. He is supposed to have said, 'Sovereigns who are born on the throne can be beaten twenty times and still go back to their capitals. But I can't, because I am a parvenu.'

(v) Was the turning-point the realisation by each of the Allies that the removal of one man was of greater importance than the capture of sugar islands, or the partition of Poland, or petty annexations in the Rhineland, Lombardy, or the Balkans?

Reading list

G. BRUUN, *Europe and the French Imperium*, Harper & Row, 1969.

D. G. CHANDLER, *The Campaigns of Napoleon*, Weidenfeld & Nicolson, 1967.

G. LEFÈBVRE, *Napoleon*, Routledge, 1969.

F. MARKHAM, *Napoleon and the Awakening of Europe*, E.U.P. 1954.

G. RUDÉ, *Revolutionary Europe*, Fontana, 1964.

J. TERRAINE, *The Big Battalions*, History Today, June, 1962.

J. M. THOMPSON, *Napoleon Bonaparte: His Rise and Fall*, Blackwell, 1951.

6 What were the most enduring of the reforms of the Revolutionary and Napoleonic periods?

The immediate, or at least the first, interpretation of this is roughly—think of the reformatory measures carried out in France by the various French Revolutionary assemblies and by the Consular and Imperial governments of Napoleon.

Having done that, you may find that there are rather a lot. Now comes the problem of organisation: how are you going to present all this material without it appearing to degenerate into a mere memorised list? You could, for instance—

1. Present them chronologically, making the obvious
   twofold subdivision   Revolutionary
                                   Napoleonic

2. Organise them under sub-headings like

           political
           economic
           religious
           legal

3. Evolve a sort of order of merit, or, as in this case, order of endurance. (How long is 'enduring'?)

4. Distinguish between

   reforms deliberately conceived and carried out by the government, like the 83 *Départements*, the local government measures.

   reforms which just 'happened' without prior planning, like the great surrender of feudal privileges on August 4th, 1789.

   reforms, or at any rate changes, which took place over a period of years. For instance, this period saw a tremendous development in the machinery for controlling public opinion

   > negatively, through censorship, spies, informers, and secret police.
   > positively, through propaganda and state educational systems.

5. Evaluate enduring reforms which turned out well for the dignity, freedom, security of man, and those which didn't.

There are probably plenty of other ways, none of which has any absolute claim to rectitude or excellence. This is where your own judgment comes in. You may well see fit to dismiss the five suggestions above as worthless. But whatever you do, you should impose *some* discipline on your material. You must give the impression that you are in charge of your facts; you must try and avoid your essay becoming a breathless recital of dates, events, and measures.

Bring your judgment to bear, too, on the following suggested examples of enduring reforms. They are offered in no special order of time, size or endurance. It is for you to decide priorities.

(i) The Declaration of the Rights of Man and of the Citizen, adopted on August 26th, 1789. Not strictly speaking a reform, in that it expressed hopes rather than decreed actions; but worth a mention, possibly because of the following reasons:

It was the general principle in conformity with which the National Assembly intended to overhaul the entire system of French government.

Along with the American Declaration of Independence, it provided the inspiration for all nineteenth-century liberals.

It was such an explicit, unequivocal denial of the whole *raison d'être* of the *ancien régime*.

(ii) Do not forget the three reforms suggested above.

The abolition of feudal privilege.

The overhaul of local government, which involved contributions from the National Assembly, the Jacobins and Bonaparte.

The improvement of the means of influencing and controlling public opinion.

(iii) Finance.

Consider the importance of

the abolition of indirect taxation by the Constituent Assembly.

the institution of improved methods of tax-collection, especially under the Consulate and Empire.

the foundation of the Bank of France in 1800.

(iv) The painstaking and thorough codification of French law, hammered out under the relentless supervision of Bonaparte.
(v) The Church.
How would you rank the enduring importance of

the Civil Constitution of the Clergy.

the great transference of Church land to peasant pro-prietors.

the Concordat with the Papacy arranged by Bonaparte.

(vi) Education.

The *Ecole Polytechnique* founded by Carnot.

The inauguration of the principle of state responsibility for, and control of, education (over thirty years, in-cidentally, before the British Government saw fit to make its first contribution to the same cause—a laughable £20,000).

The founding of the University of France, to supervise all primary, secondary, and further education.

(vii) The *levée en masse*, which gave Europe its first glimpse of a nation in arms, of total war.
(viii) The career open to talent, which had made possible the careers of men like Carnot and Bonaparte in the first place. Did the restored Bourbon regime and the Orleans monarchy mean the return of mediocrity to high places, or did the reforms in law and education keep the avenues of promotion open to everyone of merit?
(ix) How long did the Revolutionary Calendar last?
(x) Did those eager *fédérés* marching to Paris produce the most enduring reform of all, the *Marseillaise*, or does that dis-tinction belong to the ingenious device for improving the efficiency of capital punishment allegedly invented by Dr. Guillotin?

Bear in mind that historical interpretation is very seldom a matter of blacks and whites; you may find it necessary to make provisos, admit discrepancies, allow exceptions.

For example

1. Whatever became of democracy when the National Assembly had limited the franchise before the end of 1789?
2. How much 'liberty' was there in the days of the Revolutionary Tribunal or Fouché's secret police?
3. What was left of 'equality' after the inauguration of the new Imperial aristocracy?
4. Did 'fraternity' survive the Vendean risings, the White Terror of 1815, the June Days of 1848?
5. Was the Empire's poor record in the arts and letters a denial of the great 'reform' of freedom of thought promulgated so earnestly by the early revolutionaries?
6. Was the *ancien régime* really reformed out of existence when it was able to return in 1815 with such vigour, in the shape of the *émigrés* and their rancid creed of revenge?

You must also have some idea of what constitutes a reform.

Does it necessarily have to have praiseworthy results, or is the praiseworthy intention enough to qualify it?

Does it have to be a deliberate, constructive measure, or would simple abolition of a proved evil count as a reform?

Is there any moral implication? Fouché, for instance, might well have reformed his secret police, and overhauled his informer system to make it more efficient.

So is the criterion simply greater efficiency?

Supposing, say, the French system of roads and canals developed and improved noticeably between 1789 and 1815, would that be a 'reform'?

Now go back to the beginning for a minute. Consider—are there any other interpretations you could place upon the question to enable you to cast your net more widely for material?
For instance

(i) Is there any reason for restricting the question to France? If you do not thus restrict it, two enormous fields of investigation are immediately opened up.

1. The internal history of every other country during the same period, which would therefore include such interesting possibilities as

   Pitt's great overhaul of English government, or part of it anyway.

   the presidencies of Washington and Jefferson.

   the last years of two famous 'enlightened despots', Joseph II and Catherine II.

   the early years and ambitious schemes of Tsar Alexander and his 'unofficial committee'.

2. The history of French dominion in Western Europe, when Belgians, Dutch, Germans, Spaniards, Swiss, Italians (even Egyptians!) got a whiff of the revolution, a glimpse of equality, a taste for efficiency.

   Consider the effects of that on liberal and national movements of the nineteenth century.

(ii) Is there any reason for restricting the argument to reforms in the governmental sense? Suppose you take 'reform' to imply also 'development of man's knowledge', 'deepening of man's insight', 'intensification of man's awareness', or whatever . . .

   The slave trade was abolished in the British Empire, and promises were given at Vienna to extend the ban further.

   The treaties of Chaumont, Paris, and Vienna saw the beginning of an experiment in the science of the international regulation of human affairs.

   Were Adam Smith, Turgot and Pitt showing the way towards a liberation of commerce from the stifling cocoon of petty tariff?

   Lagrange (incidentally the first professor of mathematics at the *Ecole Polytechnique*) perfected the metric system of weights and measures.

Consider the impact of these men in their respective worlds.

Monge and Laplace and mathematics.

Lamarck, one of Darwin's predecessors, and botany/biology.

Cuvier, Ampère, Lavoisier and science.

James Watt and industry.

Jeremy Bentham and political economy.

Beethoven's Eroica Symphony and the classical school of Haydn and Mozart.

One last reminder. Remember you are being asked to *evaluate* various reforms.

Remember too what it is about these reforms that you are being asked to evaluate:

NOT   merit   (though these are incidental, they are)
        scope   (not, in this question, fundamental.   )
        complexity
        modernity

BUT   permanence, durability.

Reading list

A. BIRNIE, *An Economic History of Europe, 1760–1939*, Methuen, Revised 1951.
A. COBBAN, *A History of Modern France*, Vols. I & II, Pelican, 1965.
H. A. L. FISHER, *Napoleon*, Oxford, 1967.
A. GOODWIN, *The French Revolution*, Hutchinson, 1966.
G. LEFÈBVRE, *The French Revolution, 1789–93*, Routledge, 1962.
G. LEFÈBVRE, *The French Revolution, 1793–99*, Routledge, 1964.
G. LEFÈBVRE, *Napoleon*, Routledge, 1969.
F. MARKHAM, *Napoleon and the Awakening of Europe*, E.U.P. 1954.
A. MAUROIS, *A History of France*, Cape, 1960.
C. A. PHILIPS, *The Church in France, 1789–1907*, 2 vols. S.P.C.K. 1929, 1936.
G. RUDÉ, *Revolutionary Europe*, Fontana, 1964.
J. M. THOMPSON, *The French Revolution*, Blackwell, 1943.
J. M. THOMPSON, *Napoleon Bonaparte: His Rise and Fall*, Blackwell, 1951.
E. L. WOODWARD, *French Revolutions*, Oxford, 1934.

7 Was the Congress of Vienna an unqualified failure?

Beware of the implication in questions worded like this, or at least what you may think is the implication, viz:—that the Congress *was* a failure, and that you are merely being asked to explain to what extent it was a failure. Never allow your mind to be jockeyed into one particular line of thought simply because of the way the question is worded.

Do not misunderstand—the wording of the question matters and must be thoroughly grasped. But once that is done, keep the mind as open as possible.

For example, there are at least four ways of tackling this question:

Either (i) Yes, it was an unqualified failure, because of so and so.
Or   (ii) Yes, a failure, but not unqualified, because of so and so.
Or   (iii) No, a success, except for so and so.
Or   (iv) No—on the contrary, it was an unqualified success, because of so and so.

Your starting point is obviously the actual terms of the settlement. Any reputable text book will give you an adequate summary oj them. Make yourself conversant with them before reading these observations.

1. War had been raging almost continuously for twenty-three years; nearly every European nation had been involved; an unprecedented amount of property and territory had changed hands during that time; every representative at Vienna expected to get terms favourable to his government. The fact that there was a settlement at all is some evidence of success.

2. France, considering she had started it all, was let off lightly.

   Her eastern frontier could have been torn to shreds.

   Every colony could have been wrung out of her.

   Her own art treasures could have been ransacked in retaliation.

3. Note how France was practically encircled by means of the 'buffer state' idea.

The strengthening of Holland by the addition of Belgium.

The award of Rhenish territory to Prussia.

The guarantee of Swiss independence.

The re-emergence of Bavaria, largely subservient to Austria.

The control by Piedmont of Genoa and Savoy.

The re-affirmation of the Spanish Pyrenees frontier.

It could perhaps be argued that France was contained even on the seaward side by the British Navy, and by the terms of the settlement which enforced the dismantling of all military installations in French colonies.

4. Although every state except Turkey was represented in the negotiations, the important decisions were taken by the Great Powers, firstly because they were the 'Great' Powers, and secondly on the old principle of the smaller the committee, the quicker the work.

Somebody had to decide, and you couldn't please everybody.

This would go a long way to explain

the 'tidying up' of the map of Germany.

the rough treatment of the Poles, Belgians, and Norwegians.

(Incidentally, it was some of this rough justice which gave the wily Talleyrand an opportunity to pose as the champion of the smaller powers.

He was also to take considerable advantage of the rift that soon appeared between England and Austria on the one side and Prussia and Russia on the other, over the question of the amount of territory in Saxony that was to go to Prussia as compensation for her losses in Poland.

Is it a fault or a merit of the Vienna negotiations that the delegate of the defeated power was able to exercise such wide influence?)

5. There were huge new forces at work which could not be halted by a hundred treaties.

The growth in European population, or at least the beginnings of the great growth.

The gradual spread of industrialism, both within and beyond England (with its social implications).

The two 'ism's' which were said to have played a part in Napoleon's downfall (and in his rise, for that matter).

Liberalism

Nationalism

It is comparatively easy to see the strength of these forces from the vantage point of the mid-twentieth century. Are the Vienna peacemakers to be blamed for not seeing them so clearly?

And even if they did, how could they have framed an international treaty settlement to cater for them?

6. A lot of the less conspicuous work of the Congress proved to be more lasting than the terms dealing with huge cessions of land.

For example

The new rules of diplomatic etiquette and procedure to govern future conduct of international relations.

The doctrine concerning international rivers.

The settlement of the property claims of individuals who had suffered during the war.

The declarations by France, Spain, Holland, and Sweden on the slave trade.

7. The months of negotiation gave rise to two concepts which played a large part in international relations, for the next twenty or thirty years at least.

The Holy Alliance	Is it the fault of the Congress that this manifesto of utopian sentimentality, which nobody except the Tsar took seriously, was later used as a label to tag the reactionary policies of the Eastern Powers?
The Congress idea	Do the Powers deserve praise for formulating the most advanced theory of international government the world had yet seen, or do they deserve blame for not making it work?

'Failure' is a purely relative term anyway.

(i) For example, failure in the short run or the long run?

Was it Vienna's fault

that the Neapolitans rose in 1820 against the corrupt regime of the Bourbons reimposed after the execution of Murat?

that the Spanish revolutionaries' demand for the 'Constitution of 1812' produced an international crisis?

that the Belgians revolted in 1830 against partisan Dutch government?

that Italian patriots chafed for nearly half a century at Austrian domination of Lombardy?

that the Poles refused to accept the suzerainty of Tsar Alexander, despite his self-conscious 'enlightenment'?

(ii) Then again, how long is the 'long run'?

Does the Congress deserve credit for Europe's freedom from large-scale war until the Crimean fiasco, or is the forty years' peace a testimony to the diplomatic skill of men like Metternich and Palmerston? Or even to general European exhaustion after the Napoleonic Wars?

Is it true that there was no great war for a century because the Powers, by and large, were *reasonably* satisfied with the Vienna settlement?

(iii) Or, thirdly, the Congress settlement can be considered a failure *and* a success, both at the same time—depending on your point of view.

Was Alexander pleased with it?

Did Talleyrand regard it with satisfaction?

What were Castlereagh's views on his efforts at peacemaking?

All this may be regarded as playing with words, when the real job to be done is to answer the question. True, up to a point. But you must state a case; you must produce an argument. And it is suggested that any of the above lines of thought should provide a framework on which to build that argument.

Perhaps the most obvious method of all is to examine the reason for summoning the Congress in the first place. What were the delegates concerned to do?

To stop the fighting.

To restore the Balance of Power.

To contain France.

To prevent a repetition of a career like Napoleon's.

To re-establish the 'rules of the game'—the *ancien régime* concepts of diplomacy, limited wars, and hard bargaining by heads of state over the conference table, and a ruling *élite* that knew no frontiers.

(Metternich and Talleyrand were by birth, breeding and inclination, eighteenth-century aristocrats. To them, Napoleon was a parvenu, both socially and politically. His empire was an artificial growth with no claims to or likelihood of permanence. Talleyrand, for instance, was engaged in secret dealing with the Hapsburgs behind Napoleon's back as early as the Erfurt Conference.)

A familiar verdict on the Congress of Vienna employs phrases like 'putting back the clock'. But it is perhaps not unnatural that the delegates should seek their inspiration not in the foregoing twenty-three years of turmoil, but in the preceding century of relative quiet.

The *ancien régime* may not have been liberal, but at least it had been stable. And as far as the delegates could see, what had 'Liberty, Equality, Fraternity' done for Europe except plunge it into war?

Reading list

R. ALBRECHT-CARRIÉ, *A Diplomatic History of Europe since the Congress of Vienna*, Methuen, 1966.

H. KISSINGER, *A World Restored*, Weidenfeld & Nicolson, 1957.

H. NICHOLSON, *The Congress of Vienna*, Methuen, 1946.

L. C. B. SEAMAN, *Vienna to Versailles*, Methuen, 1955.

D. THOMSON, *Europe since Napoleon*, Longmans, 1957.

C. K. WEBSTER, *The Congress of Vienna*, Thames & Hudson, 1963.

8 Explain the breakdown of the Congress System

If you tackled this straight away, and produced a series of reasons for 'the breakdown of the Congress System', it would constitute an answer—of sorts. But by so doing you could well be betraying the shallowness of your learning and your lack of critical insight.

In the first place, the 'Congress System' is a convenient phrase used in text books to refer briefly to the series of international disputes and negotiations in the fifteen years or so following the Napoleonic Wars. In order, it is hoped, to make the period intelligible (and easily memorised for exams?) a good deal of 'simplification' takes place—even, the purists would say, distortion. The fact is, as any reputable study of the period will tell you, there was no such thing as a 'Congress System', any more than there was any such thing as Bismarck's 'System of Alliances' or a 'feudal system'. It is an invention not of history but of historians, along with terms like 'Renaissance' and 'Middle Ages'. So if you answered the question on the assumption that there really was a system of congresses, you would doubtless get a lot of names and dates right, but your answer would be superficial because it would show no proper understanding of the misconceptions about the 'Congress System'. You would be giving the game away that you hadn't read very much.

And in the second place, questions are often deliberately worded in such a way that you are tempted, invited, expected to query the assumptions implied in them—in addition to, or in the course of, answering them.

For example, take the question about Germany: 'Why was liberalism a comparative failure in 1848?' The suggestion is that liberalism was not a *total* write-off. But you may decide from your study of the topic that it was. Well, say so.

Or again, 'The great tragedy of the French Revolution was the war'. The implication to be immediately queried is that the war *was* the 'great tragedy', or indeed a tragedy of any size. But there's a second implication which also needs to be considered if not refuted—the suggestion that the Revolution did 'have' a 'great tragedy'. You may be of the opinion that the Revolution wasn't a tragedy, or didn't 'have' a 'great tragedy' at all. Well, once again, don't be afraid to say so.

There is a danger here, though—or rather a temptation. It is very easy to say airily, 'There was no such thing as . . . ' whatever it was, and to hope that thereby you are displaying your originality of mind, your keen ability to cut through the maze of misconception and prejudice which has hitherto masked the problem in hand, and misled generations of historians. Contentious opinions, the same as conservative ones, need logical argument and factual illustration if they are to have any force, any cogency. It is a mistake to rely solely on their shock value.

And when you say, 'There was no such thing as . . . ' just what are you refuting—the facts, or the labels applied to them? Clearly there were some congresses. So in this case it's not the facts which are at fault, but the labels. Even then, you should not sneer too much; you've got to call it all something. As Marc Bloch, a great medieval historian, put it in his *Feudal Society*, 'Provided that he treats these expressions merely as labels sanctioned by modern usage for something which he has yet to define, the historian may use them without compunction. In this he is like the physicist who, in disregard of the Greek, persists in calling "atom" something which he spends his time in dividing.'

. . . 'something which he has yet to define'—there's your clue. Make it quite clear what you understand by 'Congress System', and you can use the term as freely as you like.

For example, was it

(i) Simply the period between the first congress and the last. Examine each of the congresses,

> Vienna 1815
> Aix-la-Chapelle 1818
> Troppau 1820
> Laibach 1821
> Verona 1822

and say why they failed, or at least why there weren't any more.

(ii) The history of intervention to prevent revolutions. That was why the last three congresses were summoned, and there would probably have been more if Canning had not explicitly disowned the whole idea. So you would have to consider the effects of the various revolutions.

> E.g. Naples
> Spain
> Portugal
> Piedmont, all 1820–1821.

In this context, examine the convenient corollary later added by England—the idea of intervention to prevent other people intervening.

>E.g. Spanish America, 1823
>Portugal, 1826.

(iii) The history of the Quadruple Alliance, signed at Paris on 20th November, 1815, by which the four Great Powers bound themselves to maintain, by armed force if necessary, the arrangements of Chaumont, Vienna and Paris, for twenty years.

Article VI made provision for 'meetings at fixed periods' to discuss matters of 'common interest'.

The terms of this definition could easily be made to include

>settlement of the Belgian question.
>establishment of Greek independence.
>even the imposition of peace in the Eastern Mediterranean.

In other words, three striking examples of international consultation to prevent war—and with success.

Whatever else Metternich, Castlereagh, Canning and Palmerston may have done, they all worked to prevent European war—the great danger alike to British commercial health and Hapsburg territorial power.

(iv) The 'career' of the Holy Alliance.

After all, it was the doctrinaire interpretation placed upon its woolly aims by the Troppau Protocol in December, 1820, that made irrevocable a split already begun by Castlereagh's famous Memorandum of May.

This could stretch the scope of the question to

>1833 and the Declaration of München grätz.
>1853 and the breaking of the Austro-Russian entente.
>1872 even, and Bismarck's talk of reviving the Holy Alliance. The same old common factor was there—a union of the three eastern autocracies against revolution.

Of course you have to stop somewhere, and common sense indicates that you don't write a diplomatic history of Europe from the Congress of Vienna to the *Dreikaiserbund*. But you have to combine intelligent judgment with judicious illustration to arrive at a final date; there are almost as many dates for the collapse of the Congress System as there are for the fall of the Roman Empire. (That is, if you think it necessary to have a final date.)

Now decide the relevance of the following observations:

(i) The two congresses which produced most international co-operation were Vienna and Aix-la-Chapelle—both primarily concerned with the status of France.

After 1818 France was no longer a threat to the security of Europe. The last three congresses gave rise to or widened the rifts between certain Powers.

Is there necessarily any conclusion to be drawn?

(ii) Metternich and Alexander did not have to justify their policies to anyone; Castlereagh and Canning were responsible to an elected body of representatives.

(iii) Metternich, we are told, enjoyed some kind of personal ascendancy over the temperamental Alexander.

(iv) England, because of her commercial and imperial pre-occupations, and thanks to her insulation from the Continent by the Channel, was not so vitally involved as the other Powers in Europe's political problems. Europe simply did not matter so much.

(v) Canning did not intervene to help the Spanish rebels in 1823, but he did to help the Portuguese liberals in 1826.

(vi) Castlereagh, the patient, often reviled architect of peace, strove to work with Metternich; Canning, the bustling, brash dealer in epigrams, set out to break Metternich's hold on the diplomatic initiative.

(Compare, too, Palmerston's remark on his new Quadruple Alliance of 1834: 'I'd like to see Metternich's face when he reads our treaty.')

(vii) Except in order to deal with Napoleon, the Powers never intervened together anywhere.

> E.g. In Greece—England, Russia, France.
>
> In Naples and Piedmont—Austria.
>
> In Spain and Portugal—France, England.
>
> In Poland—Russia.
>
> In Belgium—France, Holland, England.

What would be the reason for this:

> ideological disagreement?
> lack of sea power?
> sheer distance?

(viii) Where England participated

> Portugal
> Belgium
> Greece
> South America

> the liberals/nationals succeeded.

Where she did not

> Naples
> Piedmont
> Spain
> Poland

> they failed.

(ix) The Allies at Paris swore to keep the peace for twenty years. In the event, no war involving all the Powers occurred for a hundred years. And that war was caused not by having too few congresses/ententes/alliances, but too many.

Reading list

R. ALBRECHT-CARRIÉ, *A Diplomatic History of Europe since the Congress of Vienna*, Methuen, 1966.

F. B. ARTZ, *Reaction and Revolution, 1815–1832*, Harper & Row, 1934.

H. KISSINGER, *A World Restored*, Weidenfeld & Nicolson, 1957.

H. NICHOLSON, *The Congress of Vienna*, Methuen, 1946.

H. G. SCHENK, *The Aftermath of the Napoleonic Wars*, Routledge, 1947.

H. TEMPERLEY, *The Foreign Policy of Canning*, Cass, 1966.

M. WALKER (Ed.), *Metternich's Europe*, Harper & Row, 1968.

C. K. WEBSTER, *The Congress of Vienna*, Thames & Hudson, 1963.

C. K. WEBSTER, *The Foreign Policy of Castlereagh*, G. Bell, 1931.

9 Did Alexander I make the greater contribution to Russian or to European history?

Your reading for this essay ought to include a biography of Alexander and a history of Russia. In case you should feel that such banal advice is an insult to the intelligence, the following comments may help to justify it.

In connection with this essay, you could well hear remarks like 'So-and-so's history of Europe has a jolly good section on Russia; it tells you all the main points' or 'So-and-so's notes on European history gives you the facts on Russia; it doesn't waffle'. Either way it is felt that one has collected all the main information and has thereby obviated the necessity to look at all those detailed books which 'waffle' a lot. History teachers as a rule would tend to discourage this view as somewhat narrow. When pressed for reasons, they might put forward any or all of the following:

(i) You are now taking history at 'A' Level, not 'O' Level; this demands rather more than the collection and memorising of the 'main points' from a neatly-departmentalised general history. And you've only got the author's word for it that they *are* the main points. The chances are that he's not a specialist on Russia anyway.

You should have reached the stage by now where you can appreciate the historian's gifts and weaknesses—balance, prejudice, clarity, selectivity, etc.—and where you can apply such skills of your own as analysis, judgment, criticism.

(ii) Nobody is suggesting that you have to read all these detailed works from cover to cover. There are ways and means of extracting what you want from a book without reading right through it.

Look at the publisher's blurb on the cover.

Pick out certain topics from the index.

Read the chapter headings, page headings, etc.

See what the author says about his own book in the preface.

Skim through it, look at the first sentences of paragraphs, keep your eyes open for key names, dates, ideas, etc.

(iii) Perhaps more important, a specialist work on Russia, even if it adds little to your existing factual knowledge, should (if it's any good) present history from Russia's viewpoint, not Europe's. You should gain from your reading, albeit slowly, an appreciation of Russia, a collection of impressions which should enable you to interpret and understand other things you find out about Russia in other books and concerning other periods.

For instance, how many general histories of Europe or 'notes' on European history have the space to discuss things like:

The effects of sheer size on Russian character, government, foreign policy, etc.

The apparent paradox of the crushing indignity of serfdom and the willingness of peasant soldiers to die in their tens of thousands for 'Mother Russia'.

The validity of the European verdict on Alexander I as a mysterious man.

The 'typical' Russian, in a country which embraced a bewildering variety of races, creeds, and nationalities.

The importance, to the Russians, of the other two-thirds of their country which did NOT face Europe, but which stretched towards such 'remote' places as Persia, Afghanistan, India, Mongolia, Korea, Alaska.

Whatever you choose to read, however, find out what you can about the following:

(i) Alexander himself

His birth and upbringing.

His relations with his fearsome grandmother, Catherine the Great.

His complicity in the murder of his father, Tsar Paul.

His views on his 'mission' as the father of his people.

His resolution during the crisis year, 1812.

The rumours concerning his desire for abdication and the solitary life.

His death and the legend of Taganrog.

(ii) The duality, the paradoxes, the contradictions, that surround Alexander:

The young prince destined to assume the most rigid autocratic power in Europe had his education supervised by a Swiss republican.

His early reading and study embraced authors as varied as Tacitus and Gibbon, Machiavelli and Locke.

From his earliest days he had to commute between two mutually jealous and suspicious households, those of his father, the Crown Prince Paul, and of his grandmother, the Empress Catherine.

He is associated with both liberalism and reaction.

He was only one-eighth Slav, yet he was the most popular Tsar in history.

He gave power and authority (admittedly at different times) to liberals like Speransky and reactionaries like Arakcheev.

To Europe he was the impenetrable autocrat who conned the monarchs into signing the Act of the Holy Alliance; to Russia he was the charming, open-handed, accessible, deeply-concerned father of his people, Alexander 'the Blessed'.

Several books, you may find, will go to great trouble to try and reconcile the contradictions, to prove that Alexander was really being 'consistent' throughout. If these explanations deepen your understanding of Alexander, well and good. But do all a man's actions have to be made consistent with some concocted theme in order to become intelligible? Is man a consistent creature?

(iii) The various themes that recurred, or were ever-present, during Alexander's reign:

Serfdom.

The spread of Western ideas to Russia, especially through the medium of soldiers and officers on campaign.

Russia's role as champion of the Orthodox Church.

The great debate on Russia's destiny.

E.g. Was Russian patriotism compatible with absorption of Western ideas?

Had Peter the Great's tremendous efforts represented a great leap forward into modern Europe, or a temporary aberration from Russia's true Slavonic development?

Should the Russian language be 'purified' or 'modernised'?

Russia's advance westwards.

Via the Baltic, Peter's 'window on Europe'.

Via Poland, which enabled the Tsar to be arbiter of central Europe.

Via the Black Sea, the Balkans, and the Mediterranean, which caused such flutters of alarm in Constantinople, Vienna, Paris and London.

The Tsar's self-imposed duty as protector of Europe against revolution, at a time when Russia's enormous (apparent) power, her opposition to Turkey, and her infiltration beyond the Danube were a standing inspiration to Slav nationalism. (Another Alexandrine paradox.)

Russia's eastward expansion.

(iv) Domestic affairs.

The 'unofficial committee' of Czartoryski, Stroganov, Kochubey and Novosiltsov, and their ambitious schemes for reform.

1803, the Free Cultivators Law.

1803–07, the gradual re-shaping of central government.

The reforms (projected, fulfilled, modified) of the universities.

Alexander's ideas on a constitution, and on decentralisation.

The emancipation of serfs without land in the Baltic provinces.

The finances, and the effects of the war against Napoleon.

Russian economy, and the effect on it of, say,

the Armed Neutrality
Bonaparte's Continental System
the costly wars
a very small, and politically unconscious, middle class.

The military colonies in the provinces of

Novgorod
Mogilev
the Ukraine.

Speransky's reforms as governor-general of Siberia.

The mutiny of the Semeonovsky regiment in 1820.

Arakcheev's censorship and secret police.

Poland, and the results of Alexander's attempts to give it constitutional government.

the Decembrist Conspiracy.
It happened after Alexander's death, but was he in any way responsible?

(v) Foreign affairs.

1. The legacy of Paul

     The Armed Neutrality

     Relations with Prussia.

     The interest in Malta.

2. Relations with France.

     The build-up of the Third Coalition.

     Campaigns, 1805–07—Austerlitz to Friedland.

     The treaty of Tilsit, 1807.

     The break-up of the Franco-Russian alliance, 1807–12.

     The invasion of Russia, and Alexander's part in inspiring national resistance.

     The Fourth Coalition and the liberation of Europe.

3. The Congress of Vienna.

     Alexander, as the only monarch who directly formed and controlled his own foreign policy, and whose armies and territories were far and away the largest, must have had considerable influence on the decisions taken.

4. The Holy Alliance.

     Alexander's original intention.

     Metternich's later re-interpretation.

5. The Congresses.

     Aix-la-Chappelle
     Troppau
     Laibach
     Verona

6. The Greek War of Independence.

7. Other campaigns in/involvements with

> Finland
> the Aland Islands
> the Caucasus and Transcaucasia
> Persia
> Turkey
> the Ionian Islands

8. Relations with

> Japan
> U.S.A.

When you pull the threads of your argument together to decide where you think lies Alexander's 'contribution', avoid saying something like: 'Therefore it can be seen that Alexander made the greater contribution to Russian history.'

It is usually considered bad technique to answer the question in a single sentence.

Reading list

E. M. ALMEDINGEN, *The Emperor Alexander I*, Bodley Head, 1964.
R. CHARQUES, *A Short History of Russia*, Phoenix House, 1962.
L. KOCHAN, *The Making of Modern Russia*, Pelican, 1963.
B. PARES, *History of Russia*, Cape, 1955.
N. V. RIASONOVSKY, *A History of Russia*, Oxford, 1963.
H. SETON-WATSON, *The Russian Empire, 1801–1917*, Oxford, 1967.
L. STRAKHOVSKY, *Alexander I of Russia*, Williams & Norgate, 1949.
D. M. STURLEY, *A Short History of Russia*, Longmans, 1964.
I. YOUNG, *Alexander I*, History Today, May, 1961.

The omission of works devoted exclusively to the campaign of 1812 is deliberate. Two or three are suggested at the end of Question 4.

10 Explain the reasons for the collapse of the restored Bourbon Monarchy

You are doubtless aware of the historical truism that every regime contains within itself the seeds of its own decline. Common sense in any case would dictate that an examination of the fifteen years from 1815–30 ought to produce most of the required answers.

An obvious starting-point is the restoration itself, or rather the restorations—both of them.

In 1814 it was a negotiated affair. Paris gave Louis an enthusiastic welcome.

Then came Louis' undignified flight.

In 1815, it was imposed on the French.
Louis XVIII, returning, as all the books say, 'in the baggage-train of the Allies', personified the national humiliation of Waterloo. (Incidentally, the peace terms were more stringent too.)

Could you make anything out of that comparison?

Alternatively, start at the other end with the 1830 Revolution, and then go back to try and explain it. This is not to suggest that you turn the essay completely on its head, and reverse all chronology. It is meant only to be a possible starting point. It is quite common practice to search for something dramatic by way of an opening, and in that sense the revolution itself can legitimately be put to that purpose.

Thirdly—it is possible to make a case that the Bourbons could have got off to quite a good start.

E.g. Most Frenchmen welcomed peace.

Talleyrand's work at Vienna secured France's re-entry to the Concert of Great Powers.

The Bourbons were the one group of possible rulers whom nobody actively feared.

Everyone was prepared to compromise a little in what everyone hoped in 1815 was a return to sanity and normality.

The extraordinarily quick financial recovery secured the payment of the war indemnity by 1818.

So, what went wrong?

1. Well, take the phrase 'restored Bourbon Monarchy'. Even after the revolution of 1830, the French tolerated another monarch for 18 more years, so perhaps the trouble was not that the regime from 1815 to 1830 was monarchical, but that it was Bourbon.

Louis XVIII   Fat, indolent.

Intelligent enough to see that the system he personified, however shaky, would see him out. Rather a negative view of government, perhaps.

Charles X   A creature of the *ancien régime*, so steeped in its philosophy as to be almost unaware of what had happened since 1789, certainly incapable of compromise with it.

What, for example, do the books associate with Louis and Charles?

The insistence on dating the new reign from 1795.

The claim that the Charter of Liberties ought to proceed from Royal generosity.

The business about the tricolour.

The shooting of Marshal Ney.
Every new regime, especially a restored one, has its vendettas and witch-hunts, which people are prepared to tolerate up to a point. Take the Terror of Reaction after the fall of Robespierre, or the revenge on the English regicides in 1660. But, when looking for a *political* scapegoat, to fall upon the darling of the Army, the hero of Moscow, the 'bravest of the brave', to shoot Ney—of all people!

The attempt to revive the Divine Right of Kings.

Charles' insistence on a full coronation at Rheims, with all the trimmings.

> The appointment as War Minister of Bourmont, the traitor of 1815. The new Minister of the Interior was La Bourdonnaye, the man identified with the White Terror.
>
> Charles' obstinacy in appointing, and persisting with, Jules Polignac, whose grandiose schemes of foreign expansion threatened to undermine the peace of Europe, never mind the throne of France.

Any single one of the above is hardly likely to topple a government on its own, but put together, they do appear to indicate a lack of tact and common sense on the part of Louis and Charles, on a scale big enough to make an outside observer throw up his hands in despair. What must it have done to Frenchmen at the time?

2. What else came back with the restored Bourbons?

The *Emigrés*	Consider their behaviour, and its effect on French society. If you and your family, after centuries of wealth and privilege, had lost land, fortune and position in undignified flight; and then returned after twenty-odd years' exile convinced that God was at last favouring the just, how would you behave?

The protagonists of the traditional power of the Church, the Ultramontanes.

3. Consider the threat of the above to

> the great landownership changes of the Revolution.
>
> the Concordat of Napoleon.
>
> the new freedom won for secular education by the Revolution and enshrined in the great Codes.

4. Ask yourself who had most cause to feel hard done by as a result of the new regime.

> E.g. The Jacobins, republicans, reds, revolutionaries, the left, or what you will.

Had the ideals of the Great Revolution been betrayed?
More to the point, did these radicals *do* anything about it?

The Bonapartists.
All those civil servants, 'new' aristocrats, unemployed
soldiers, officers on half-pay—did *they* do anything about
it?

The Orleanists.
After all, their candidate had once fought for the Revolution at Jemappes.

Were these groups in command of sufficient strength or resources
to topple a government?

5. Was it the Bourbon genius, second only to that of the Stuarts
(Charles II of England excepted), for alienating that vast centre-
section of moderate public opinion that is usually prepared to
give any regime the benefit of the doubt—to begin with at any rate.

Note the parallels.

Stuarts and Bourbons blindly cherished Divine Right.
The crime perhaps was not so much that it was wrong as that
it was out of fashion.

The passion for corrupt and inept favourites.
It would make an interesting argument to decide who was
worse—Carr and Buckingham, or Decazes and Polignac.

The religious bigotry.
Charles I pushed the Prayer Book down the throat of the Scots.
Charles X restored the Jesuits and made sacrilege a capital
offence.

The impractical waste of time and effort on wild schemes of
foreign expansion.

Charles I's futile Spanish expeditions.
Polignac's harebrained Belgian plot.

The refusal to accept clear statements of public opinion
expressed through publicly elected assemblies.
Compare the Stuarts' dissolutions of Parliament with Charles
X's 'cavalier' treatment of the Assembly in 1830.

The constitutional inability of either to compromise.

C. V. Wedgwood's remark about Charles I of England in *The King's Peace* could be applied equally well to his Bourbon namesake: 'When he thought a cause was good he would not yield, and by "not yielding" he did not mean that he would yield on sufficient persuasion, or the day after tomorrow, or the year after next; he meant that he would not yield.'

6. Is it necessary to look beyond politics?

Karl Marx may have been wrong on some things, but he had a point when he drew attention to the economic factor in history.

So what would you look for?

> Slumps?
> Unemployment?
> High food prices?
> The social evils attendant upon the gradual spread of industrialism from England to France?

To go back for a moment to the opening paragraph, about 'seeds of decline'. You must be prepared, in your examination of a regime like this, to come up against facts which, at first sight, don't fit. To put it another way, not *everything* you discover about the Bourbon regime will necessarily be a symptom of decline, or a reason for failure. The worst regimes have their good points. (Even Mussolini got the trains to run on time, so we're told.)

Ideally, perhaps, it should be evident in your essay that you are aware of these good points. So how do you mention them without weakening your overall argument?

One suggestion is based on the cards principle of playing your losing tricks first.

> E.g. .... 'Although the Bourbons can take a measure of credit for so-and-so, this was totally outweighed by their stupidity in so-and-so.'

You are still directing the reader's attention to the mistakes; that is what forms the main clause of the sentence; that is the last thought that you leave with him. It is more effective than saying...

> 'The Bourbons made a mess of so-and-so, but they did well to sort out so-and-so.'

Same facts, different presentation.

Remember you are not being asked to cheat; merely to present an argument, to make a case.

Then there are the facts which *appear* not to fit the argument, but which, with close scrutiny and careful handling, can still be put to use.

For example

    (i) The French Navy was successful at Navarino in 1827. Why would this not have helped the Bourbons?

   (ii) Success attended French armies in the Spanish expedition of 1822–3—something which had eluded all Bonaparte's armies in the Peninsula for six years.
But what sort of King was restored to power? And who led the troops—the Duc d'Angoulême or Marshal Moncey?

  (iii) A new colonial empire was being built in North Africa, Senegal and Madagascar.
How did Algerian tribesmen and African 'natives' compare as opponents with the might of the Prussian army at Jena and Auerstädt or the Russian hordes in the snow at Eylau?

Now what could you make of the following?

    (i) The assassination of the Duc de Berri in 1820.

   (ii) The Emperor, having spent most of his time dictating memoirs, died in 1821.

  (iii) The government's proposed compensation for *émigrés*.

  (iv) The disbandment of the National Guard in 1827.

   (v) Retired generals, as is their wont, started publishing their war memoirs.

  (vi) A new generation was growing up in France as distant from the 1789 revolution as the present sixth-form generation is from the Second World War.

 (vii) Historians were now getting to work on the Great Revolution
        e.g. Thiers
            Mignet.

Does all this produce a complete answer? Does it explain why Charles X, after his apparent coup with the July Ordinances, was in England by the beginning of August?

Who or what provides the clue?

>
> Polignac?
> Lafitte?
> Talleyrand?
> The radical Left?
> The Paris barricades?

As always, at the end of an essay, try and get further back from the canvas you have been examining so that your eye can take in the whole picture. Never get too engrossed in piling fact on fact simply to impress on the examiner what a learned scholar you are.

Look at the whole regime; does anything strike you?

> Was it the Bourbon mistake to concentrate on nationalist aspirations and to ignore liberal ones?

> There appeared to be little active opposition to the Bourbons in the country at large. Was it rather that the Bourbons made so little impression on French life that nobody noticed or bothered when they went?

> Was it the Bourbons' long exile which left them completely out of touch with every aspect of French life and thought?

> Was it that Frenchmen felt the age of opportunity was gone? With God and the Emperor all things were possible; how many field-marshals' batons were there in soldiers' knapsacks now?

> Perhaps it was the Bourbons' mistake to be not wrong but dull.

Reading list

F. B. ARTZ, *Reaction and Revolution, 1815–1832*, Harper & Row, 1934.

D. W. BROGAN, *The French Nation, 1814–1940*, Hamilton, 1957.

J. P. T. BURY, *France, 1814–1940*, Methuen, 1969.

J. H. CLAPHAM, *Economic Development of France and Germany, 1815–1914*, Cambridge, 1936.

A. COBBAN, *A History of Modern France*, Vol. II, Pelican, 1965.

J. GARSTON, *The British in France, 1815–18*, History Today, June, 1961.

N. E. HUDSON, *Ultraroyalism and the French Restoration*, Cambridge, 1936.

M. D. R. LEYS, *Between Two Empires: French Politicians and People, 1814–48*, Longmans, 1955.

A. MAUROIS, *A History of France*, Cape, 1960.

C. S. PHILIPS, *The Church in France, 1789–1907*, 2 vols, S.P.C.K. 1929, 1936.

J. B. WOLF, *France, 1814–1919*, Harper & Row, 1963.

E. L. WOODWARD, *French Revolutions*, Oxford, 1934.

11 Show how the Zollverein came about, sketch its history, and estimate its contribution to German unity

You probably know the time-honoured excuse of historians for not knowing the answer to a question—'It's not my period.' So students, according to their disposition, either laugh wryly at their teacher's regrettable limitations, or fulminate self-righteously about the evil effects of excessive specialisation.

But the joke has two sides. The other half concerns the student who says 'We don't have to know that because it's not in the syllabus'. This retort, or a variation on it, might well be the reply to the suggestion that a brief study of the background to a topic might assist towards an understanding of it.

In this case, some acquaintance with a few of the main features of previous German history might help the student to get the Zollverein in perspective. Now do not misunderstand. Nobody is suggesting for a minute that you devote as much time to the century before the syllabus period as you do to the syllabus period itself. Use your common sense. But there are ways and means of collecting information on a topic's historical environment without ploughing through specialist tomes.

You can glean all sorts of worthwhile material from

(i) Collections of essays by historians, distinguished and otherwise. Some are listed at the back of this book.

(ii) Book reviews—in the Sunday papers, 'History Today', 'Times Educational Supplement', and so on. Reviews often contain all sorts of general comment and useful argument. A review of, say, a book on the Austro-Prussian War of 1866, could quite possibly begin with a paragraph summarising the course of and reasons for Austro-Prussian rivalry since 1740.

(iii) Opening chapters of specialist books, which are often devoted to setting the scene, describing the background, putting the subject in perspective, or whatever. Such chapters are inevitably over-simplified and somewhat generalised, but that is exactly what you want.

(iv) Radio and television programmes. Because they are geared for the general public, they can be, and often are, superficial in their treatment of particular topics. But their very simplicity and superficiality can sometimes make clear an issue which no specialist book has seen fit to spell out for you.

(v) Even the big encyclopaedias—dry, factual, dull probably. But within their limitations, accurate and reliable. And they do always 'do' the whole topic, from the year dot.

(vi) In fact, almost anything might make something occur to you —museums, films, historical novels, picture galleries, and so on.

Perhaps most important, having collected odd scraps of information, or having had a new idea occur to you, WRITE IT DOWN. DON'T just say 'oh, that's interesting; I must put it in an essay sometime'. You won't; you'll forget. Nobody's memory is as good as he or she likes to think it is.

However, suppose for a minute that you have obediently collected all sorts of background material for the Zollverein. How are you going to place the Zollverein in its historical context? Here are three suggested introductions:

(i) The growth of the Zollverein fitted into the general process of overhaul that Prussia was being put through by Stein, Scharnhorst and Hardenberg.

> After administrative
>   educational
>   military
>   agrarian
> and municipal reforms
>   economic reform was a natural corollary.

(ii) The Zollverein marked the beginning of Germany's recovery from the economic stagnation into which she had fallen at the end of the Middle Ages.

> The era of the great discoveries caused a shifting of the commercial axis of Europe from the Centre to the West.

> E.g. Venice and Genoa declined.

> So therefore did the South German cities dependent upon their trade.

> The Hanseatic League gave way before the greater resources of the Atlantic powers.

> The sixteenth-century Wars of Religion tore Germany apart.

The Thirty Years' War left permanent scars on Germany's trade, cities, agriculture, and population.

In the eighteenth century the disintegration process reached its height, with over 300 separate states, and with the two great dynasties of Europe, Bourbons and Hapsburgs, both concerned to keep Germany disunited.

(iii) The Zollverein is another step in the gradual process of Prussia's rise to dominance in and over Germany.

> E.g. 1640–88 Frederick William, the Great Elector, architect of Brandenburg-Prussia, and founder of the military tradition.
>
> Frederick I raised his electorate to the status of kingdom.
>
> Frederick II (1740–86) used the army built by his dreadful father, Frederick William I, to challenge the might of the Hapsburgs, and survived.
>
> Stein, Gneisenau and Scharnhorst built the new Prussia over the ashes of Jena and Auerstädt, and it was Blücher's Prussians who tipped the scale at Waterloo.
>
> And so on, through to Bismarck.

Be careful here; because an historian can detect a trend, a theme—in this case Prussia's rise from obscure impoverished electorate to hegemony of all Germany—it doesn't follow that people could see it at the time. Do not attribute too much conscious shaping of history to its participants. Because Bismarck had built the German Empire by 1871, it doesn't follow that he had worked out a timetable of war and annexation in 1862, and ticked off each item like a shopping-list.

The essay itself is comparatively straightforward. It is even worded in such a way that a simple threefold treatment is the obvious and best method.

1. How did it come about?

(i) Consider the 'historical climate'.

> E.g. The ideas of Turgot and Adam Smith.
>
> The gradual spread of the Industrial Revolution.

The natural anxiety of the Prussian reformers to gain a share in the huge new wealth that was flowing to and from Britain, and, later, Belgium and France.

(ii) Examine the problems facing the rulers of post-war Prussia.

The sprawling territories.

How to encourage trade in a country which bordered on 28 others and which had 67 internal tariff barriers of its own.

How to produce a thriving economy to make up for Prussia's political dominance by Austria.

How to provide an outlet for the corn from their eastern provinces.

The beguiling possibilities of

a unified system of weights and measures,
a universal coinage, and so on.

2. The history of the Zollverein.

Any reliable history of nineteenth-century Germany will give a reasonable outline. You should examine topics like

Maassen's Tariff Reform Act.

The first customs union.

Other customs unions besides the Prussian one.

The constitution of the Zollverein.

The Zollverein's methods of inducing other states to join.

How many states were part of the Zollverein by, say, 1850.

The Zollverein's attitude to Austria.

The commercial treaties with foreign powers, i.e. non-German.

The disputes between the free traders and the protectionists, between the agriculturalists and the industrialists.

The renewal of the Zollverein in 1853.

3. The Zollverein's contribution to German unity.

   (i) Consider the importance of a unified fiscal direction of Germany.

   (ii) Look up a few figures for things like

        imports and exports
        industrial output
        mileage of new roads and railways.

        How much of that would have been due to the Zollverein?

   (iii) By increasing so much contact between Germans for the good of Germany (or at any rate Prussia), how much German 'consciousness' did it instil?

         Perhaps the very attempts of Austria to undermine it, and Prussia's rigid discipline of it, are a testimony to the importance the two great rivals attached to it as a means of dominating Germany.

   (iv) Did it get Germans into the mental habit of imagining a Germany without Austria?

   (v) Do not forget to set the importance of the Zollverein against that of other agencies working towards German unity. For instance

        The spread of the railways.

        The Bund (or was that a centrifugal force as a result of Metternich's work?)

        The Prussian bureaucracy.

        The Prussian army (though you might work out how many military successes it achieved between 1815 and 1866).

        Bismarck, obviously.

Austria, by default.

The authoritarian tradition of Prussian government.

The Hegelian ideology of the all-powerful State.

Remember, the question did say 'estimate' the Zollverein's contribution; so you must make it clear that you are aware of the other unifying factors.

Reading list

J. H. CLAPHAM, *The Economic Development of France and Germany, 1815–1914*, Cambridge, 1936.

R. FLENLEY, *Modern German History*, Dent, 1968.

W. O. HENDERSON, *The Zollverein*, Cass, 1968.

H. HOLBORN, *A History of Modern Germany, 1648–1840*, Eyre & Spottiswoode, 1965.

J. A. R. MARRIOTT and C. G. ROBERTSON, *The Evolution of Modern Prussia*, Oxford, 1946.

E. J. PASSANT, *A Short History of Germany, 1815–1945*, Cambridge, 1959.

K. S. PINSON, *Modern Germany: its History and Civilisation*, Collier-Macmillan, 1966.

A. J. P. TAYLOR, *The Course of German History since 1815*, Hamilton, 1948.

12 'La France s'ennuie'. How accurate a comment is this on the July Monarchy and its failure?

The examiners have decided that they are going to set a question about France between the years 1830 and 1848. So the simplest thing to do would be to frame something like this:

'Write down all you know about the reign of Louis-Philippe.'

However, the examination is designed to test something rather more than memory. The candidate should be able to demonstrate his capacity to organise facts, to present an argument.

So why didn't the examiners say something like:

'Explain the reasons for the downfall of Louis-Philippe.'

Well, for one thing, the chances are they've already done it in one or two other questions, so they have to ring the changes a bit.

For another, they are anxious to test other historical skills:
e.g. the capacity to

> weigh facts
> make critical comment
> question accepted theories
> discern trends
> speculate imaginatively.

So they come up with a quotation, the validity of which you are invited to discuss. Do not make the mistake of accepting it blindly, and mangling the evidence to fit it. Do not make the equally danger-ous mistake of trying to be clever: that is, do not try to demonstrate your independence of mind by tearing the theory to shreds, which might involve equal distortion of the evidence.

These quotations are merely the means of entry into a discussion of the relevant topic. There is no implicit suggestion that they are right or wrong, or even partially right or wrong. The examiners want your opinion, obviously, but it must be an opinion based not on tame acceptance, nor on factious disagreement, but on intelligent analysis of all the facts at your disposal.

So beware quotations:

> do not give a chronological account
> do not provide lists of reasons why
> do not try to be clever.

But do not be put off either. The question is still testing your knowledge of Louis-Philippe, and if you happen to know a lot about him you would be rash to reject it simply because it was unexpectedly phrased. A bit of thought, the use of plain common-sense, the jotting down of random facts, all help to provide clues.

One last suggestion. It sometimes helps, if you're stuck, to get a first paragraph down on paper even if you're not quite sure where you're going after that. Ideas have an occasional trick of falling into place only after you're actually started.

This suggestion is regarded in some quarters as heretical—the idea of actually beginning the essay without a plan or an outline at your elbow.

> Be it noted that the suggestion is being made *only* for this type of essay, and *only* if the 'outline' method fails. If the rules don't work, you make your own.

What follows is a list of some of the events, topics and personalities on which you ought to collect evidence in order to form your conclusions. It makes no claim to being either exhaustive or authoritative, but it should give you a start.

1. Louis-Philippe himself

> King by the Grace of Parliament, not the Grace of God.
>
> His odd-shaped face and unprepossessing figure—the answer to a cartoonist's prayer.
>
> His increasing intransigence with advancing age (and he was getting on when he came to the throne).
>
> His desire for an active part in politics. Is there any worthwhile parallel between Louis-Philippe, Guizot, and the 1848 Revolution—and George III, Lord North, and the loss of the American colonies?

2. The nature of the new monarchy

> What constitutional changes were made after the July Revolution?

What effect did these changes have on the strength. effectiveness, and dignity of the new regime?

What, for instance, did Frenchmen think of a King who went around with an umbrella?

How would a ruler like Tsar Nicholas regard a man who owed his throne to a few days' street rioting?

3. The various ministries of the 1830s

Lafayette, Lafitte, Casimir-Perier, Soult, Broglie, Molé, Thiers.

Finally, Guizot, whose rule lasted longer than anyone's. Does he deserve credit for producing stability, or does he incur odium for clinging feverishly to power?

4. Foreign affairs

Belgian revolt.
Carlist wars in Spain.
Quadruple Alliance.
Wars of Mehemet Ali and his son Ibrahim.
Pritchard incident in Tahiti.
Spanish Marriages.
Polish revolt.
Election of a liberal Pope, Pius IX.
War of the cantons in Switzerland.
Completion of the conquest of Algeria.
Revolt in Palermo (January, 1848).

Does the Orleans regime have a good record in its conduct of foreign affairs?

If not, what could it have done better?

5. The Napoleonic Legend

1830   the Bonapartists did not even make a bid for power.

1832   the Duke of Reichstadt died.

1833   Thiers produced his *History of the Consulate and Empire*.

1836   Louis Napoleon's first feeble attempt at a *coup d'état*.

1836   The Arc de Triomphe was completed.

1840   Louis Napoleon tried again, and failed equally dismally.

1840   the Emperor's remains were re-interred in the Invalides.

What conclusions might be drawn from that?

Is it useful to make a distinction between the apparent weakness of the Bonapartist party and the apparently growing appeal of the Legend?

6. Religion

Because of the rabid Ultramontanism of the 1820's the Church took a lot of knocking in the 1830's. For instance, Catholicism ceased to be 'the religion of the State', and became the religion 'professed by the majority'.

How burning an issue was the clerical and anti-clerical feud during the rule of Louis-Philippe?

7. Education

Did Guizot's encouragement of education and insistence on professional qualifications for secular teachers help to inculcate a sound appreciation of law and order in the young, or was the end product of his work a new generation, better informed and more critical of the regime?

8. The Economy

How fast was the Industrial Revolution spreading in France?

What were the good and bad results of the railway boom in the middle forties?

Was the level of production rising in keeping with population? In other words, was the standard of living going up or down?

Were the forties in France as 'hungry' as they were in Britain?

9. Reform

(i) The things that attracted the attention of reformers

the franchise

the corruption of the electoral machinery.

the personal conduct of men in high places (revealed by a series of celebrated scandals).

the social evils attendant upon

overcrowded urban life.
over-zealous capitalistic expansion.
the mechanising of industry.
the bad harvest and potato blight of 1845–6.
prices and wages generally.

(ii) The reformers

Every shade and variety of radical opinion

Utopian socialists like Saint-Simon and Fourier. (The writings of both pre-date 1830. What reflection is it therefore on the Orleans regime that both should be read so avidly?)

Cabet.

Louis Blanc and his 'Right to work'.
(What circumstances would have called forth a slogan like that?)

Proudhon and his view that all property was 'theft'.
(What would have driven him to that conclusion?)

Wild revolutionaries like Blanqui.

Raspail, the reforming doctor of Paris.

The more professional politicians like Ledru-Rollin, Odilon Barrot, and, coming nearer the Centre, Thiers.

Was it the regime's fault that Thiers and other Centre men found themselves drawn more and more to the Left in an effort to gain results?

Remember there was pressure on the government from the Right too.

Lamennais and his Liberal Catholicism.

The Clerical party (including the Jesuits) agitating against the 'excessive' influence of the State in education.

The sullen resignation of the Legitimists.

The Olympian disdain of the old landed gentry, who, debarred from the Upper House by the decree suppressing the hereditary peerage, retired to their country estates.

(iii) Reformers' activities

E.g. Industrial riots in Lyons.

The political propaganda of newspapers like *L'Avenir, National,* and *Reforme.*

Anti-clerical riots in Paris.

Banquets and barricades.

10. Paris

Cultural centre of Europe.

Haven of political refugees from all corners of the continent.

Mother of revolutions.

What really determined the fate of French governments—the opinion of France or the opinion of Paris?

Now, having collected your information, you must decide how much of it, if any, supports the contention of the question, that France was 'bored'. How far was Lamartine right? (He was the one who said it, actually.) What reliance should you place on the remark of a poet who tried unsuccessfully to be a politician, and a remark, incidentally, made in 1839, not 1848.

Is there anything more shrewd or accurate in the verdict of another contemporary, de Tocqueville? He observed that the government in 1848 was not 'overthrown'; it was 'allowed to fall'. Does this in fact reinforce Lamartine's idea that France was bored, apathetic?

If you cannot find verdicts like this from authoritative sources, do not be afraid to suggest one or two of your own.

For example

Was France 'frustrated'?

> The Left nearly got their republic in 1830, and were thwarted at
> the last minute by the craftiness of Talleyrand, and the con-
> venient union of a second-string monarchist with the hero of the
> Great Revolution, Lafayette. Louis-Philippe was a stop-gap, a
> last hope. Is there any comparison between the sense of dis-
> appointment and frustration felt by the republicans after 1830,
> and that experienced by the British lower classes after the
> shortcomings of the 1832 Reform Act became known?

Was France 'purposeless'?

What did the Orleans regime stand for?

> > Empire?
> > Republic?
> > Monarchy?

> What did it believe in, apart from the self-perpetuation of Guizot's
> upper-bourgeois oligarchy?

A final thought.

As has been suggested in another section, do not be too wise after
the event. Because a regime ultimately failed, it does not follow that
everything pointed towards its failure.

In the case of the Orleans regime, for example, nobody was more
surprised than the banqueteers when a programme of agitation
designed to remove a single minister culminated in the overthrow of
an entire system of government.

What had the Orleanists to fear?

> Legitimism was discredited after 1830.

> Jacobinism was still almost a dirty word.

> Bonapartism gained no ground from the fiascos of 1836 and
> 1840.

If the Orleans monarchy had succeeded, doubtless the historians
would have come up with all sorts of political, economic, social, and
religious reasons for its success. (Remember the speed and completeness of the 1848 revolution staggered everybody.)

To use an example from earlier French history. . . . Bonaparte, by all the rules, should have lost the Italian campaign of 1796

his army was starved, badly clothed, ill equipped.
morale was low.
the Austrians were confident of success.
the French Government was corrupt.
the Revolution had gone sour.
Bonaparte himself was only 27, a nobody on the European stage.
he was short, had long hair, spoke with a Corsican accent, and was generally unprepossessing.
his passionate love-letters to an unfaithful gossip of a wife made him the laughing-stock of Paris.

If Bonaparte had lost, the historians could well have used some of the above reasons, and many others, in order to explain it.
Yet Bonaparte won.
So he must have had something. What? He wasn't quite sure himself. Indeed, it didn't dawn on him till half-way through the campaign that he had something special.
To apply the illustration to the Orleans monarchy therefore—did it fail because of all the customary reasons—economic, political, social, or whatever? Or did it fail because it *lacked* something special? If so, what?

Reading list

D. W. Brogan, *The French Nation, 1814–1940*, Hamilton, 1957.

J. P. T. Bury, *France, 1814–1940*, Methuen, 1969.

J. H. Clapham, *Economic Development of France and Germany, 1815–1914*, Cambridge, 1936.

A. Cobban, *A History of Modern France*, Vol. II, Pelican, 1965.

M. D. R. Leys, *Between Two Empires: French Politicians and People, 1814–48*, Longmans, 1955.

A. Maurois, *A History of France*, Cape, 1960.

C. S. Philips, *The Church in France, 1789–1907*, 2 vols., S.P.C.K. 1929, 1936.

J. Plamenatz, *The Revolutionary Movement in France, 1815–71*, Longmans, 1952.

J. B. Wolf, *France, 1814–1919*, Harper & Row, 1963.

E. L. Woodward, *Three Studies in European Conservatism*, Cass, 1963.

E. L. Woodward, *French Revolutions*, Oxford, 1934.

13 Metternich has been called a reactionary. Why?

History has a trick of identifying certain people with certain ideas or events.

E.g.

Richard the Lion Heart—the Crusades.

Robespierre—the French Revolution and the Reign of Terror.

Similarly, Metternich—reaction.

It should be your purpose, therefore, to examine the processes which have produced this particular identification, taking the opportunity *en passant* to offer comment on the logicality and fairness of those processes.

Well, what has produced this identification?

The 'label' habit of writers, this passion that some of them have to stick simple tags to people, to reduce everybody to a slogan?

The verdict of contemporaries?

Metternich's view of himself?

Partiality in selection of evidence?

The cumulative, and overwhelming, effect of all the available facts?

In each case, use your own judgment and common sense.
For instance

(i) 'Labels' have their uses, as long as you bear in mind their limitations. It is reasonable to assume that Metternich must have been reactionary in some ways, otherwise the association of the word with his name would never have been made in the first place.

But reactionary in every way?

Or again, 'reactionary' is a derogatory term. Can *nothing* be said for Metternich?

(ii) Contemporaries' verdicts have the value of immediacy, and, often, personal acquaintance.

But immediacy and personal acquaintance do not necessarily imply accuracy or fairness.

Castlereagh, for example, thought Metternich was something of a buffoon; Bonaparte dismissed him as an intriguer; German liberals regarded him as the agent and personification of everything they hated.

People who pass remarks about others often reveal as much of themselves as they do of the people they are judging—even more perhaps. (The Convention in Paris once passed a solemn motion that William Pitt was 'the enemy of the human race'. What does that tell you about William Pitt?)

(iii) Like many people with a long career in politics and in the public eye, Metternich said, and wrote, a good deal about himself. How do you disentangle self-revelation from self-deception?

He said, amongst other things, that

he never had a 'system'.
he had often ruled Europe, never Austria.
he had been born at the wrong time.
he should have lived either in the eighteenth century, before Europe contracted the fell disease of 'revolution', or in the twentieth, when (presumably) it should have recovered from it.

(iv) Selection of evidence, or at any rate the attitude to evidence, often varies according to the society, and the times. A distinguished Dutch historian, for example, has written a book not about Napoleon, but about the changing verdicts of historians *on* Napoleon. (P. Geyl: *Napoleon, For and Against*.) Professor Butterfield has made a similar study of the historiography of the reign of George III, *George III and the Historians*.

Suppose you, the present judge of Metternich, live in a society which accepts the principles of the rights of man and of national self-determination. What is going to make your view of him any more valid than that of someone, say, who enjoyed a privileged position in Tsarist Russia, or who now lives under, and supports, the present regime in South Africa?

(v) Students are, for the most part, unable to study the documents; they have to rely on what are called 'secondary authorities'—in other words, books. But books can be informative if you have used your initiative beforehand to cast your net wide.

In the case of Metternich, for example, the stereotyped picture concerns his 'rule' of post-war Europe. But Metternich was already forty-two in 1815, already old enough to resent writing the new digit in the date for the new year. He himself regarded his great days as over. So search his earlier career too. Is there any worthwhile comparison between Metternich, and that other survivor from the *ancien régime* who made a living in post-war Europe—Talleyrand?

Now collect material on Metternich's attitude to, dealings with, responsibility for, achievements in, the following:

(i) His various diplomatic posts before becoming Chancellor.

(ii) The marriage between Napoleon and Marie-Louise.

(iii) The war against Napoleon.

> Wagram and after.
> The Fourth Coalition.
> Negotiations with Napoleon in 1813 and 1814.

(iv) The various treaties and consultations which marked the end of the war.

> Chaumont
> Paris
> Vienna.

(v) The Holy Alliance.

> Distinguish between Metternich's early attitude to it, and his later re-interpretation of its doctrines and purpose.

(vi) The Congresses.

> Aix-la-Chapelle, and the re-instatement of France.
> Troppau, and its notorious Protocol.
> Laibach, and the treatment of Ferdinand of Naples.
> Verona, and the dispute with Canning.

(vii) Italy.

The return of Austrian power to Lombardy.
The secret police and the Carbonari.
The revolutions of 1820 in Piedmont and Naples.
The revolutions of 1830–31.
Mazzini and the 'Young Italy' movement.

(viii) Germany.

The Bund.
The Zollverein.
Kotzebue and Karlsbad.
The 1830 revolutions.
The Austro-Prussian rivalry for German leadership.

(ix) The Eastern Question.

The Serbian revolt.
Greek Independence.
Russia's entry to the Mediterranean.
Russia's intrusion into the Balkans.
Slavonic nationalism generally.

(x) Russia.

Alexander's change of mind from admiration of Napoleon,
to open opposition.
Again, Alexander's conversion from mystic liberalism to
reflex hatred of revolution.
Austria's relations with Tsar Nicholas.
The agreement at Münchengrätz.

(xi) The various confrontations with England.

The revolt of the Miguelists in Portugal.
The independence of Spanish America.
The Belgian revolt.
The Carlist wars in Spain.
The annexation of Cracow.
The dispute among the Swiss cantons.

(xii) The July Revolution in Paris, and the bourgeois monarchy
of Louis-Philippe.

(xiii) Obviously, the 1848 revolution in Vienna.

Now assess the value of the following random comments on Metternich:

1. Europe, after 1815, needed, above all else, peace. This, by and large, was what Metternich helped to provide. In that sense he was in tune with his times.

2. The real reactionaries in Vienna were the Emperor himself, Francis, and Metternich's great rival for his ear, Kolovrat.

3. Metternich's great crusade (or rearguard action, depending on your point of view) against revolution was really a colossal confidence trick. By keeping the King of Prussia and the Tsar in a constant state of nerves about 'the revolution', Metternich was able to

   divert Prussia's attention from the leadership-of-Germany issue.

   preserve the mouth of the Danube as Austria's lifeline, free from a Russian stranglehold.

   It was a feat of political *légerdemain* comparable to that (much later) of Bismarck, who attempted another great triple alliance when he knew perfectly well that Austria and Russia, if their territorial ambitions came out into the open, were bound to become enemies.

4. Metternich was modern enough to have thought of a 'German' league, even an 'Italian' one.

5. The trouble with Metternich was that he never tried to make things happen; he was always trying to stop them happening. Ultimately, like Louis-Philippe, he was negative, and therefore, a failure. Oddly, he was cynically aware of this himself. He knew that the days of the life he represented were numbered.

6. Metternich put his faith in institutions, not individuals, because they were tougher, and lasted longer. He was vindicated by Waterloo; he had known that Napoleon, however clever or powerful or terrifying, would ultimately fail or die because he was mortal. The Hapsburg dynasty, the Established Church, the government bureaucracy, would survive, and save society.

   It is hardly surprising that a man of mature years who had seen his point so conclusively proved should continue to govern his behaviour by the same philosophy.

7. As soon as industrial technology produced a successful proletarian movement, and thus a fluid, egalitarian society, it was also able to provide the machinery and means of communication to control it. But a proletarian movement and a fluid egalitarian society *before* these controls were available would have lapsed into anarchy. It was this great 'truth' which Metternich strove to put across to his colleagues and rivals in the art of government.

Now, how much of all this is relevant?

In a subject of this nature it's very much a question of how much of it you can make relevant. You are being invited to talk about Metternich. Well, talk about him. If you work out the plan of your essay thoroughly, and word your sentences carefully, you can get a great deal of all this to relate to the topic.

And don't be afraid to let the discussion wander now and then, so long as you don't let it get lost. You must always keep the main theme in sight. In this case the theme is 'Metternich as a reactionary'. And to prove that your discussion isn't lost, it is quite a good idea to return to your main theme by way of conclusion.

For example

Richard the Lion Heart, with his personal bravery, his generalship, his travels, his concern for the Holy Land, his flair for publicity, sums up in himself the virtues we fancy should belong to the true soldier of Christ. (We do not particularly want, or like, to know that he was a selfish, volatile, spendthrift, homosexual, absentee monarch who didn't give a damn for England.)

Similarly, Robespierre, with his selfless devotion to Rousseau, his utter incorruptibility, his remorseless logic in following wherever his ideals led, his inability to compromise, represents truly memorable features of the Revolution—its sincerity and its implacability.

So too, Metternich contributed to the defeat of Napoleon, he suggested sensible reforms in Austria, he maintained the Balance of Power, he helped to provide Europe with forty years' peace; but his career from 1815 to 1848 (which he himself regarded an as anticlimax) makes him forever the personification of that society which strove for so long to put the Genie of Revolution back into the bottle which had been uncorked when the mob broke into the Bastille.

Reading list

R. ALBRECHT-CARRIÉ, *A Diplomatic History of Europe since the Congress of Vienna*, Methuen, 1966.

G. DE BERTIER DE SAUVIGNY, *Metternich and his Times*, Darton, 1962.

C. DE GRUNWALD, *Metternich*, Falcon Press, 1953.

A. J. MAY, *The Age of Metternich, 1814–48*, R. & W. Holt, 1963.

L. B. NAMIER, *Vanished Supremacies*, Peregrine, 1962.

A. J. P. TAYLOR, *The Hapsburg Monarchy*, Hamilton, 1948.

M. WALKER (Ed.), *Metternich's Europe*, Macmillan, 1968.

E. L. WOODWARD, *Three Studies in European Conservatism*, Cass, 1963.

14 Why did the Turkish Empire not collapse completely in the first half of the nineteenth century?

The glib reply is 'Because nobody wanted it to'.

Unfortunately for 'A' Level candidates, examiners require a lengthier explanation. However, snap judgments like the above contain enough truth in them to be of use in framing a fuller answer.

Another possible starting-point is the famous comment about the 'sick man of Europe'. Explain why the Ottoman Empire, by all the rules, *should* have collapsed, and then show why it didn't.

Or, thirdly, take an episode from the close of the eighteenth century—the Oczakov affair, 1791—and use it

to show that the 'Eastern Question' goes back before 1800.

to illustrate some of the themes which remained fairly constant from 1800 to 1850.

E.g. Russian expansionism to the South-West.

England's concern at Russian entry to the Mediterranean.

You then apply similar treatment to the other incidents which involved Turkey and the Powers after 1800.

The incidents which require study are roughly as follows:

1. The Russo-Turkish wars

Intermittent since the days of Peter the Great.

More dangerous (to Turkey) with the growing power of Russia under Catherine the Great and Alexander I   1768–74.
1787–91.
1827–29.

2. The Russo-Turkish treaties

1774 Kutchuk-Kainardji.
1792 Jassy.
1829 Adrianople.
1833 Unkiar Skelessi.

3. The last Partition of Poland (1795)

> Having filled one 'power vacuum', Austria and Russia turned their attention, and rivalry, to the next—Turkey.

4. Nationalistic revolts against Turkish overlordship

> The Serbs in the 1800's.
> The Greeks in the 1820's.

5. The activities of Mehemet Ali and his son Ibrahim

> 1824 Ibrahim in the Morea.
> 1827 The Navarino episode.
> 1832 Ibrahim's conquest of Syria.
> 1830–40 Mehemet's attempt to gain full independence.

6. The various international gatherings and agreements relating to the matter of Turkey

> | | |
> |---|---|
> | 1822 The Congress of Verona | (The Greek question) |
> | 1826 The St. Petersburg Conference | ,,   ,, |
> | 1827 The Treaty of London | ,,   ,, |
> | 1831 The London Conference | ,,   ,, |
> | 1833 The Convention of Kiutayeh | (Ibrahim in Syria) |
> | 1840 The Treaty of London | (Mehemet's revolt) |
> | 1841 The 2nd Treaty of London | ,,   ,, |

Why were the affairs of a non-Christian, out-of-date, proverbially corrupt (even by contemporary standards), ramshackle regime like the Ottoman Empire of such absorbing interest to the European Powers?

Be careful to distinguish between excuses and reasons.

> E.g. The Tsar chose the occasion of the Greek revolt to make pious pronouncements about his protectorship of all Greek Orthodox Christians under Ottoman rule (a claim he had concocted, quite unfairly, from a tiny clause in a treaty nearly fifty years old).
>
> Metternich, also concerned with Greece, uttered equally pious platitudes about maintaining 'legitimate' Turkish rule in her European territories, when the Hapsburg-Ottoman feud had been a constant factor in European politics since the sixteenth century.

Napoleon took a host of philologists and archaeologists to Egypt with him, but he took a pretty sizeable army too.

The Greeks' struggle, with its evocation of the glories of Hellas, may have stirred English hearts in the 1820's, but Canning did not intervene simply because a club-footed poet died at Missolonghi.

N.B. This does not mean that excuses had no truth or value at all. They may have been genuine enough.

Alexander *was* concerned about his co-religionists.

Metternich *was* committed to the doctrine of legitimacy.

Napoleon *was* interested in Egyptology.

But they were often expressed in exaggerated form to divert attention from more wordly or less unselfish motives.

What then were the real interests of the Powers in the Eastern Mediterranean, the interaction of which served to preserve the integrity of the Ottoman Empire?

1. Russia

Territorial expansion	Peter the Great had gained his 'window on Europe' by extending Russian rule to the Baltic.
	Catherine II had pushed Russia into Central European politics by annexing nearly half Poland.
	The next step was expansion South-West towards the Mediterranean. (Catherine's first two grandsons were not christened Alexander and Constantine by pure coincidence.)
Economic factors	Control of the mouth of the Danube.
	Access to the Dardanelles.
	Tapping the resources of the Balkan grain lands.

Religious factors   It is worth repeating that the Tsar was the champion of the Greek Orthodox Church.

What prevented the Russians from going ahead?

Austrian rivalry in the Balkans.

Alexander's soul-searching over the Greek revolt

To interfere to support his co-religionists?
Or to suppress a liberal revolt in the name of the Holy Alliance?

The certainty that England would not tolerate Russian entry into the Mediterranean. England's navy was beyond arguing with.

So Russian foreign policy underwent a change; the 'frontal attack' method was modified:

Mehemet Ali was not encouraged, on the grounds that it would be far easier to infiltrate and influence the Ottoman Empire as it stood. If Mehemet should overturn the Sultan and become master of the Empire, his efficient rule would present a far stronger barrier to Russian designs.

A good deal of Russian attention was also diverted to the 'back door' of the Empire—the Caucasus, Turkestan, Persia, Afghanistan.

2. Austria

Metternich had no wish to see the loose Turkish overlordship of the Balkans superseded by a militant Russian one.

Moves towards national independence, as shown by the Serbs and the Greeks, were not to be encouraged; they were dangerously apt to serve as examples to the subject races of the Hapsburg Empire.

Metternich was against all popular movements anyway, and believed in the maintenance of the *status quo* at almost any price. Such a policy also enabled him to keep the diplomatic initiative in Europe.

3. England

The maintenance of the Turkish Empire was vital to the English concept of the Balance of Power, in the Near East.
The trade routes to India must be protected at all costs, whether from
> French imperialists like Napoleon,
> Russian crusaders like Alexander,
> or Egyptian adventurers like Mehemet Ali.

(In the eighteenth century, the English Government was especially touchy about its West Indian possessions; by the nineteenth century, the most sensitive spot, the jewel in the crown, had become India.)

4. France

Napoleon had started it with his grandiose schemes to destroy England's Indian Empire.

By fishing in the troubled waters stirred by Mehemet Ali, France hoped to be able to take advantage of any situation he provoked.

Now that much of her empire in India and the Americas was lost to England, France was slowly building up a new sphere of influence in North Africa. The 1820s saw French troops campaigning in Algeria.

That France enjoyed little success in this area was due largely to
> Palmerston
> the British Navy
> the pacific nature of her minister Guizot.

Going back for a moment to the opening paragraph, it was suggested that the short, snappy answer sometimes has its uses in directing enquiry.
'Why did the Turkish Empire not collapse?'
'Because nobody wanted it to.'
It is hoped that the above comments help to explain why.
It is also worth bearing in mind, for this and for many other questions too, that the obvious answer may provide an idea or two—on the lines of 'Why-did-the-chicken-cross-the-road? To-get-to-the-other-side.'

'Why did the Turkish Empire not collapse?'
'Because it wasn't weak enough.'
E.g. Sultan Mahmoud attempted in the 1830s to pull Turkey up to date.

> Western ideas were introduced.

> Commercial treaties were signed with England and other countries (another reason, incidentally, for England wishing to maintain Ottoman integrity).

> Von Moltke started reorganizing the Turkish Army (the beginnings of the German connection).

The Ottoman Empire, like its Hapsburg rival, drew strength from its very weakness.

> Mixtures of race, language, and religion prevented co-ordination among subject states.

> The primitive systems of education and communication, and the apathy produced by centuries of corruption and exploitation, made organised rebellion just as difficult as organised government.

Again, like the Hapsburg Empire, the Ottoman Empire had been 'there' for such a long time that it was difficult to make the mental effort to imagine the world without it.
Both empires, like Charles II, were an unconscionable long time a-dying.

Finally, is this stereotyped picture of Ottoman decadence a fair one?

Or is it purely the legend which has grown out of the shocked gossip of foreign observers brought up in the tradition of what they like to think is Western efficiency?

'All that we hear about the decay of the Turkish Empire . . . is pure and unadulterated nonsense.' At least that's what Palmerston thought. And he was in a position to know—wasn't he?

Reading list

M. S. ANDERSON, *The Eastern Question, 1774–1923*, Macmillan, 1966.
H. DODWELL, *The Founder of Modern Egypt*, Cambridge, 1967.
E. S. FORSTER, *A Short History of Modern Greece, 1821–1940*, Methuen, 1941.
S. GHORBAL, *The Beginnings of the Egyptian Question and the Rise of Mehemet Ali*, Routledge, 1928.
P. M. HOLT, *Egypt and the Fertile Crescent, 1516–1922*, Longmans, 1966.
G. E. KIRK, *A Short History of the Middle East*, Methuen, 1964.
B. LEWIS, *The Making of Modern Turkey*, Oxford, 1968.
J. A. R. MARRIOTT, *The Eastern Question*, Oxford, 1940.
A. MOOREHEAD, *The Blue Nile*, Hamilton, 1962.
B. PARES, *A History of Russia*, Cape, 1955.
N. RIASONOVSKY, *A History of Russia*, Oxford, 1963.
R. SETON-WATSON, *England and Europe, 1789–1914*, Cambridge, 1937.
H. TEMPERLEY, *A History of Serbia*, G. Bell, 1917.
C. M. WOODHOUSE, *The Greek War of Independence*, Hutchinson.
C. M. WOODHOUSE, *The Battle of Navarino*, Hodder, 1965.

15   Why was German liberalism a comparative failure in 1848?

This is a topic in which lots of '—ism's' tend to fly about.

nationalism
liberalism
constitutionalism
socialism
particularism
dynasticism

Even

feudalism (when serfdom was abolished)
communism (Marx and Engels' famous Manifesto came out just
in time for the 1848 Revolutions).

So it would be as well to get some idea of what they all mean.
It would also pay to take a good look at a reliable historical atlas.
The map of Germany is pretty complicated even at the best of times,
and no examiner would demand a detailed knowledge of the size and
whereabouts of every state in the Bund. However, it is reasonable to
expect you to know a bit about it, say,

the size and extent of Austria and Prussia.
the importance of Hungary in Hapsburg territory.
a few bigger states like Bavaria.
the rough difference between Greater Germany and Little Germany.

A third tip—learn to distinguish the three races involved in this
question,

Teuton
Slav
Magyar.

Do not confuse them with nationalities,

> e.g. Prussian
> Bavarian
> Czech
> Hungarian
> Bohemian.

Sometimes they coincide; sometimes they don't.

Fourthly, do not jump to conclusions.

E.g. All revolts that took place in what we now think of as Germany were not necessarily German.

The reasons why the Hapsburgs survived the Hungarian revolt are not necessarily the same as the reasons why they survived the German liberal movement.

All German liberals did not want German unity any more than all German nationalists wanted liberalism.

Because the liberal movement failed in Germany, was it therefore doomed to failure from the start? Never be too wise after the event.

Now to the question. What was wrong with German liberalism?

1. German liberals, for a start.

The Frankfurt Parliament represented, and largely comprised, the intellectual, the official and professional classes.

What, you might ask, was so wrong with that?

(i) That was *all* Frankfurt represented—brains.

It did not represent

money (big business, capitalism, or what you will).

power (the Army, the Princes).

people (either rural peasantry or the embryonic urban proletariat).

(ii) The Frankfurt liberals were all, like Brutus, 'honourable men'. And, like Brutus, they made the mistake of assuming that all other men acted from motives as high as their own.

Liberals, by definition, are too reasonable, too tolerant, too nice altogether to survive in the jungle of politics without something else to back them up.
And anyway, is there such a thing as a genuine liberal revolution?

2. The Frankfurt Parliament.

It is arguable, of course, that the mere feat of summoning and assembling a democratic body to represent such liberal and national aspirations, in a country so economically backward (compared with France and Britain) and politically reactionary (the Princes), represents a major *success* in itself.

But you can still use this fact in your argument.

> E.g. It could serve as an opening for the essay, as a means of highlighting the irony of the final failure.
>
> It can be used to 'tie up' the German revolutions with others, to put it in perspective, to set the scene. Most of the 1848 revolutions began with spectacular successes which amazed even the most optimistic revolutionaries.
>
> It could also help to answer that awkward word in the question—'comparative'.
> The question is suggesting to you that there was *some* credit due to German liberals; there was *some* hope to be salvaged from the wreckage of their political experiments. So was the mere fact that a Parliament of Germany once existed, however briefly, an encouraging precedent for future liberals, nationalists, revolutionaries?
> Did 1848 provide the inspiration for the Weimar and Federal Republics, as Frederick the Great and Bismarck provided it for Kaiser Wilhelm and Hitler?

But to get back to the Frankfurt Parliament's obvious lack of immediate success.

Examine the following points, and see what conclusions can be drawn from them.

(i) The interminable debates.

(ii) The lack of effective executive machinery.

(iii) The appointment as Vicar of the Empire of Archduke John—a Prince
—and an Austrian.

(iv) The commitment to foreign politics in the Schleswig-Holstein question.

(v) Religious differences

> some deputies were Catholics
> some Lutherans
> even a few Hegelians and other religious sceptics.

(vi) The offer of the Crown to the King of Prussia in March 1849, three months *after* he had successfully crushed the liberal revolt in Berlin.

(vii) Frederick William's insulting refusal.

3. The 1848 revolutions themselves.
   There were too many of them, almost one for every state in the Bund (39). How many of these were going to be of material assistance to German liberalism:

(i) The 'economic' riots?

> bargees raided steamships.
> waggoners pulled up railway lines.
> artisans smashed factory machines.

Would these desperate men, fighting a losing battle against the new forces of *laissez-faire* and industrialism, give their support to political innovations designed, among other things, to extend personal freedom and private enterprise?

(ii) The rural revolts? (Especially in the South-West.) Once they had secured the abolition of local feudal privilege, would the traditionally conservative peasants give time or support to lofty theorising in distant Frankfurt?

(iii) Even the liberal revolts within states?

Would successful liberals in separate states be willing to jeopardise their freshly-won concessions for the sake of *possible* rights which *might* be assured by the Frankfurt Parliament if *all* the Princes agreed?

4. The unanswered questions raised.

What would be the effect of the following problems on the cause of liberalism?

  (i) What did 'Germany' mean?

       Prussia absorbed into Germany?
       Germany absorbed into Prussia?
       Germany without Austria?
       Germany with Austria, but without Austria's Slav territories?

 (ii) What about Germans *outside* Germany?
     In

       Holstein
       Alsace-Lorraine
       Courland
       Limbourg
       Some Swiss Cantons.

(iii) How could an intellectual debating society in Frankfurt persuade two dynastic military regimes like Austria and Prussia to settle their rivalry for leadership of a new Germany, a Germany moreover that was to be democratic and peaceful?

N.B. It should have become evident that points of nationalism are here being discussed rather than those of liberalism.
In the case of Germany it is very difficult to keep them apart.

     It was often state loyalties (i.e. 'local' nationalism) which bedevilled the efforts of the men of Frankfurt.

     And anyway, since the liberals of Frankfurt were concerned to construct a *united* liberal Germany, it is almost impossible *not* to mention nationalism.

     However, you could fairly be accused of wandering off the point if you then extended the argument to embrace the Slav revolts in the Hapsburg territories, and the Hungarian uprising.

5. Missing factors.

A glance at some more successful revolutions might provide a clue or two. What was it other revolutionaries had that the Germans didn't?

   (i) A central, urban, heart for the movement.
Where was the 'Paris' of Germany?

  (ii) A numerous urban proletariat.

       Look up some figures for industrial expansion and urban population in Germany.

       How many Bastilles were there to storm in Germany, and how many mobs to storm them with?

 (iii) Outside support.

       Would France be pleased to see a powerful united Germany on her borders?

       Would the Tsar be kindly disposed towards a liberal regime that might set a dangerous example to his Polish subjects?

       Did German politics really *matter* to England?

 (iv) An external threat/scapegoat/enemy to unite the revolutionaries.

       Poles, Hungarians, Italians had foreign princes to remove. Germans had to get rid of their own, to cut away part of their own heritage.

  (v) A hero, a prophet.

       Did Germany suffer from having no Mazzini, no Kossuth?

6. The opposition.

Did the cause of liberalism founder simply because there were too few liberals and too many reactionaries?

E.g. Could the liberals possibly have framed a programme to appeal to

Catholics *and* Protestants
Peasants *and* artisans
Rhinelanders *and* Bavarians
Berliners *and* Viennese
Industrialists *and* workers
Monarchists *and* republicans?

Did they really have a chance against Prussian and Austrian armies?

Lastly, remember the question did say 'comparative failure'. Did anything survive the reaction of 1849–50?

(i) As already suggested, the idea of a united Germany did. What changed possibly was not the desirability of unity, but the means of achieving it.

(ii) The abolition of many relics of feudalism was a definite gain.

(iii) Jews gained their freedom.

(iv) The middle classes thereafter took a greater and more informed interest in politics.
What are the implications of that?

(v) Princes by the dozen had been forced either to abdicate, to run away, or to grant constitutional concessions.

Their recovery of power was swift, but a precedent had nevertheless been set.

To what extent was the mere fact that a revolution had taken place in 1848 a source of inspiration to German liberals thereafter?

Reading list

G. BARRACLOUGH, *The Origins of Modern Germany*, Blackwell, 1947.

T. EDWARDS, *Vienna in 1848*, History Today, October & November, 1960.

R. FLENLEY, *Modern German History*, Dent, 1968.

J. A. HAWGOOD, *The Frankfurt Parliament*, History, Vol. XVII, 1932.

J. A. R. MARRIOTT and C. G. ROBERTSON, *The Evolution of Modern Prussia*, Oxford, 1946.

L. B. NAMIER, *1848—The Revolution of the Intellectuals*, Oxford, 1944.

L. B. NAMIER, *Vanished Supremacies*, Peregrine, 1962.

E. J. PASSANT, *A Short History of Modern Germany, 1815–1945*, Cambridge, 1959.

R. POSTGATE, *The Story of a Year: 1848*, Cape, 1956.

A. J. P. TAYLOR, *The Course of German History since 1815*, Hamilton 1948.

A. J. P. TAYLOR, *The Hapsburg Monarchy*, Hamilton, 1948.

A. J. P. TAYLOR, *Grandeur and Decline*, Pelican, 1967.

16   What common elements can be found in the revolutions of 1848?

More the 'S' Level type of question, this. Its very scope precludes any attempt at factual, chronological narrative; remember you have only about 45 minutes to produce an answer in the examination. So the examiners are looking for something else—the ability to range over a wide topic, and thereby to offer intelligent summaries, discern possible patterns, advance reasonable theories. BUT (there's always a 'but') you must not allow the discussion to be *completely* general— broad statements can become so broad as to be almost meaningless.

For instance, supposing someone wrote in an essay about the French Revolution: 'The real reason the French people revolted was that they were oppressed. They were tired of being exploited. And all people sooner or later become so exasperated with exploitation and oppression that they revolt. So the French people at last expressed their grievances which the government had done nothing about for years, and when the government still did nothing, the revolution began.'

Well, so what? Even if every syllable is true, what has it all told you? There's not one single item of fact for the memory to grasp. And it is so fatally easy to write like this, especially when you are searching for some general remarks with which to conclude an essay, and you are in a hurry to get on to the next one.

The problem is bigger here, because this essay in a sense must consist entirely of general remarks. So you have to be bold, sweeping, discursive; and at the same time you must say something definite. And it isn't easy.

Get clear in your mind first just how big a field you have to cover. Assuming for the moment that 'revolution' embraces everything from 'overturning of established government' to 'civil disturbance', there were revolutions in the following places:

1. Germany	Prussia
	Austria, in both German and Slavonic dominions.
	Nearly every state in the Bund.
2. Hungary	Magyars against Hapsburgs
	Slavs against Magyars.

114

3. Italy saw revolutions in   Turin   Florence
                                        Venice   Milan
                                        Rome   Naples
                                        Palermo.

4. France—as usual.

5. Belgium—sporadic urban riots.

6. Great Britain—the last gasp of the Chartists

                 the Young Ireland movement.

7. Switzerland—the attempt of the Catholic Cantons to secede from the Federal Union.

8. Spain—revolt in Madrid.

9. The Ottoman Empire—the attempt of the Rumans to secure 'home rule' for Moldavia and Wallachia and to join with fellow-countrymen trying to wrest Transylvania from Hungary.

Note two interesting 'absentees' from the list.

Russia, whose people were arguably the most oppressed of all.

Poland, with a tradition of gallant (if unavailing) nationalist struggle which went back to the mid-eighteenth century.

N.B. The 'common elements' set out below are put forward in the form of factual statement purely for the sake of simplicity. So you must at all times remember:—

1. They *should* be in the form of questions, or at least conjecture.
2. There ought to be phrases like 'by and large', 'generally speaking' and 'on the whole' all over the place.

3. No 'element' is likely to be completely 'common'.
4. To paraphrase George Orwell, some common elements are more common than others.
5. Your own judgment is involved. Do not accept a verdict merely because it happens to be in print. The printing-press is not the organ of revealed truth; authors are just as liable to talk rubbish at times as anybody else. Give an author due credit for his knowledge and experience, but an argument, an idea, a theory, has to make sense *to you* before you will be able to express it coherently or persuasively in an examination.

The following points are presented to form a rough chronology of the revolutions. There is no order of importance implied in this arrangement.

(i) The revolutions all had a common origin.

> The financial crisis of 1846.
>
> The bad harvests of 1846 and 1847.
>
> The cholera epidemic that ravaged Europe in the mid- and late 1840s.
>
> The hungry forties generally.
>
> The social effects of the beginnings of industrialisation.
>
> The growth of population.
>
> The improvements in transport and communication.

(ii) As Sir Lewis Namier observed, 'Revolutions are not made; they occur.'

(iii) Although the revolt in Palermo preceded that in Paris, in time, the revolutionaries all over Europe acknowledged the inspiration of Paris, the mother of revolutions.

(iv) The revolutions represented a repudiation of

> the old alliance between throne and altar.
>
> state frontiers.
>
> the Vienna settlement (its last surviving architect, Metternich, was one of the first fugitives).

(v) The revolutions were city revolutions.

> E.g. Paris
>   Berlin
>   Prague
>   Vienna
>   Budapest
>   Turin.

Little attempt was made

to involve the peasantry.

to devise a programme of social or land reform which might appeal to the peasantry.

(vi) The wrong people were leading the revolutions.

Intellectuals, theorists, poets, university dons, country gentlemen.

Men like Mazzini, Petofi, Kossuth, Lamartine, Palacký, Balcesco.

(vii) No revolution boasted unity of leadership, object, or method.

E.g. Monarchist Piedmontese v. Federalist Neo-Guelphs.

O'Connor's firebrands disgusted and finally frightened off Lovett's moderates.

Blanqui and Barbès actually led a revolt against an assembly only just elected by the whole nation.

Far from deciding on a common strategy, the Slavs couldn't even agree on a common enemy.

Turks
Russians
'Great' Germans
Hapsburgs, or
Magyars?

They never decided.

(viii) The revolutions, nevertheless, achieved initial success with unbelievable, bewildering speed. This was to lead to fatal errors and omissions.

E.g. The leaders found that, once in power, constructive statesmanship did not come as easily as revolutionary fervour.

They also, in the flush of quick success, made the mistake of underestimating the resilience of the Establishment and its ability to stage a comeback.

They failed to note, until it was too late, that the armed forces stayed loyal to the throne. And it was the troops of Cavaignac, Windischgrätz, Oudinot, and Radetsky which crushed so many of the revolts.
Even in London, the Duke was able to draft 170,000 special constables in case the Chartists should cause a disturbance.

(ix) So, thanks largely to military force, the revolutions failed.

More than that, the wheel made a full turn to produce regimes just as autocratic as before 1848.

E.g. the Second Empire

the Piedmontese monarchy

the rule of Schwarzenberg in Vienna

ultimately the triumph of Bismarck.

(x) Most of the revolutions were national rather than liberal.

Notions like universal suffrage, equality of opportunity, freedom of conscience, did not receive much attention.

(xi) The common result of the despair, pain, and frustration of failure was emigration.

America was the known haven for all religious and political minorities.

The Oregon Trail had recently opened the way across the great prairies and the Rockies to the Pacific.

In 1849 gold was discovered in California.

Look up the emigration estimates, especially for Ireland and Germany.

(xii) 1848 represented the last gasp of the idealists, the end of the tradition of secret societies and student revolts and noble gestures.

The revolutionaries of 1848, for the last time, put their faith in the power of persuasion, in the wisdom of debate, in the willingness of the 'haves' to put themselves out for the 'have-nots'.

Thereafter, the creed of revolutionary nationalism changed. If Pharaoh could harden his heart, so could the Israelites:

E.g.

The new cry in Ireland becomes 'Home Rule'.

The 'natural harmony of interests' as a fashionable creed gives way to the 'class war'.

Cavour plans to get one of the Powers to do the fighting for him.

Germany is now to be united by 'blood and iron'.

(xiii) Most of the revolutions have a remarkable dramatic unity; they happen very fast, they blaze brilliantly, and then, just as suddenly, they're gone, finished.

E.g.

The Chartists' Monster Petition was laughed out of the House.

Louis-Napoleon's plebiscite was overwhelming.

Kossuth, though he lived another fifty years, never saw Hungary again.

N.B. To repeat, the above are offered not as infallible truths, but as guides to thought and enquiry.

One last word. Do not expect to be able to fit everything you find into a particular common pattern. You will come across facts which have to be accepted and related for what they are—unique.
For example, what would you do with the fact that

the Hapsburgs abolished serfdom.

or the success of the Swiss Federal Diet represents a triumph for liberalism?

You may well of course come to the conclusion that *all* the revolutions are unique, and that this searching for 'common elements' is purely an academic exercise, with about as much practical use as selecting a World cricket team.

Remember however that the 'A' Level History Examination is intended to be an academic exercise, so you must show willing. The practical use may not lie in the field of historical scholarship, rather in providing you with a chance to display some historical skills, albeit at a fairly humble level.

Reading list

Cambridge Modern History, Vol. XI, has a chapter on the 1848 Revolutions.

R. CARR, *Spain 1808–1939*, Oxford, 1966.

G. D. H. COLE and R. POSTGATE, *The Common People*, Methuen, 1956.

R. FLENLEY, *Modern German History*, Dent, 1968.

C. A. MACARTNEY, *Hungary: A History*, Edinburgh U.P. 1962.

L. NAMIER, *Vanished Supremacies*, Peregrine, 1962.

J. PLAMENATZ, *The Revolutionary Movement in France*, Longmans, 1952.

R. POSTGATE, *The Story of a Year, 1848*, Cape, 1956.

R. W. SETON-WATSON, *A History of the Rumanians*, Cambridge, 1934.

A. J. P. TAYLOR, *The Course of German History since 1815*, Hamilton, 1948.

A. J. P. TAYLOR, *The Hapsburg Monarchy*, Hamilton, 1948.

A. J. P. TAYLOR, *Grandeur and Decline*, Pelican, 1967.

D. THOMSON, *Europe since Napoleon*, Longmans, 1957.

A. J. WHYTE, *The Evolution of Modern Italy*, Blackwell, 1944.

The list is endless, because, ideally, you need to study detailed histories of each separate country that experienced revolutionary disturbances. Time and inclination rarely permit such luxuries, so use your common sense to select the books with the widest scope, or the historians with the biggest reputations.

17 Account for the failure of Italian nationalism between 1815 and 1850

Suggested introductions:

(i) The taste of efficiency provided by French rule in Italy between 1796 and 1815. The re-imposition of the old ways afterwards was thus doubly irksome.

(ii) Murat, King of Naples, and his dream of a united Italy.

(iii) The remoteness of Italian unity in 1815.

Use the Vienna terms to illustrate that Metternich was right— 'Italy' *was* a geographical expression.

(iv) Take a particular episode which can be said to epitomise the Italian problem.

E.g. The expulsion of Mazzini and Garibaldi from Rome in 1849. Here is evidence of

political inexperience.

betrayal by fellow Italians (in this case the Neapolitans).

lack of outside assistance.

sheer lack of manpower and resources, before the might of France and Austria.

desertion by the Church.

the insufficiency of gallantry alone.

Then describe the period in question in such a way as to show that the same points recur again and again.

Make yourself familiar with the following topics:

The nature and extent of Austrian influence and power in Italy.

The Carbonari.

1820–21—the risings in Naples and Piedmont.

1830–31—the revolts in Modena, the Papal States, Parma, and
          Ferrara.

French intervention—Ancona, 1832–38.
                    Rome, 1849.

Pio Nono, Gioberti, and the Neo-Guelphs.

The career and ideas of Mazzini.

Charles Albert, Victor Emmanuel, d'Azeglio, and the 'Piedmontese' party.

1844—the martyrdom of the Bandiera brothers.

1848—the revolutions—Palermo, Naples, Piedmont, Tuscany,
                     Lombardy, Parma, Modena, Venice,
                     Rome.

1848–49—the Reaction—Custozza
                     Novara
                     Rome
                     Venice.

  Have a good look at the map of nineteenth-century Italy, and
familiarise yourself with the whereabouts of Piedmont, Lombardy,
the Romagna, Tuscany, the Quadrilateral, and so on.
  Get it clear before you start what your plan is going to be.
For example: (i) The geographical approach   Revolutions in
                                                Piedmont
                                                Revolutions in
                                                Naples
                                                Revolutions in
                                                Rome, etc.

            or (ii) The chronological method   Take each attempt
                                                at national unity,
                                                and   explain   its
                                                failure as you go
                                                along (liable to be
                                                tedious, this).

or (iii) Summarise the failures   Then arrange the
                                    explanations in
                                    one of the ways
                                    suggested in
                                    Essay 1.

The greater the amount of material at your disposal, the more difficult it is likely to be to create a clear picture and a coherent argument.

N.B. Comments are not necessarily applicable to *every* revolutionary failure in Italy; some obviously will be more relevant to particular episodes than to others.

Secondly, an observation that may apply to Italian politics in, say, the 1820s, need not be relevant to the situation in the 1840s. That is the trouble with questions like this which cover a wide period.

Why did Italian nationalism fail?
There is no attempt made here to induce you to accept any point as of greater importance than the others. Use your own judgment.

1. It was not always clear what 'Italian Nationalism' meant.

E.g. To Mazzini and his romantics, it meant the union of Italy under republican rule, the 'Third Rome', after Rome of the Caesars and Rome of the Popes.

To the Neo-Guelphs, it meant an Italian federation under Papal leadership.
But Pio Nono let them down when it came to the crunch. (As Metternich remarked, 'A liberal Pope is a contradiction in terms.')

Others wanted a loose federal organisation led from Turin.

D'Azeglio and the monarchists looked to a constitutional kingdom of Italy led by the House of Savoy.
The ultimate success of this method was due as much to the failure and discrediting of its rivals as to any intrinsic merit of its own.

2. Traditions of local sovereignty went deep. Some of the North Italian states in particular had traditions of self-government going back to pre-Renaissance days. Some of them saw little point in exerting themselves to remove the Austrians if it meant accepting the overlordship of the House of Savoy in their place.

3. Distinguish between revolutions aimed at national unity and revolts designed to secure liberal concessions from individual rulers. States which had secured the latter were not inclined to risk losing them in a nationalist crusade against the Hapsburgs.

   Sicily, for instance, wanted, not union with Italy, but separation.

   Neapolitan liberals did not profit much by going it alone. Ferdinand promised the required constitution, then ran away to Metternich, who sent him back protected with an Austrian army to crush the 'rebels'.

4. The Church, despite Pio Nono's brief flirtation with liberalism, was almost by definition a powerful champion of the status quo.

   'Fear God; honour the King.' By implication, rebellion was not merely ill-advised; it was impious.

   And the Church touched the lives of more people than Mazzini's manifestos.

5. Metternich

   The secret police, the spies, the informers, the letter-opening.

   The Austrian army (note how many revolts were put down by military force).

   No matter how much one may disapprove of Metternich's political philosophy and detached cynicism, one must concede that he was efficient.

6. Communications (both intellectual and physical)—or rather the lack of them.

   It is surely more than coincidence that neither Germany nor Italy was united until the coming of the railways.

The lack of contact was heightened by barriers of local dialect
local custom
local prejudice,
among a backward people dependent for guidance on a conservative Church which exercised enormous social influence.

The lack of any formal educational system.

It is more than likely that, far from disagreeing with the
patriots' activities, the vast majority of 'Italians' had no
genuine understanding of them.

The political theories were the pastime of the educated few.

7. Successful revolutions tend to rely on a discontented urban
proletariat, itself the product of swift industrialisation.

How many factories were there in Italy before 1848?

8. It has been observed that no revolution against foreign rule
during the nineteenth century succeeded without outside help.

The Italian nationalists enjoyed nothing except England's good
wishes.
(It was a lesson that Cavour was quick to learn.)

9. Pervading the whole period is this atmosphere of amateurism, of
tragic gallantry.

The attempts are too diffuse, too impractical, too full of symbolic
gestures.
Radetsky's troops and Oudinot's guns proved that Italy needed
statesmen, armies, and allies, not poets, prophets, and martyrs.

Romance and swashbuckle were simply not enough.

That shrewd manager of men, Florence Nightingale, regretted
after meeting Garibaldi that he was heroic but vague, and
possessed of 'no administrative capacity'.
(C. Woodham-Smith, *Florence Nightingale*.)

The most natural conclusion would be to point to the future—to Italy's ultimate success.

By 1850   The nationalists had been blooded.

> The Papacy, the Republic, the Federation, had all failed or been discredited. The way was open for the House of Savoy.
>
> In Cavour, Italy found a man prepared to fight the enemy with the enemy's methods.

Were all these failures, in a sense, necessary? Were they in a way not complete failures, but all steps, however hard, in the required direction?

Did Italy, like England in a different context, have to 'try all the wrong ways first'?

Reading list

H. ACTON, *The Bourbons of Naples*, Methuen, 1956.

R. ALBRECHT-CARRIÉ, *Italy, from Napoleon to Mussolini*, Columbia, 1960.

G. BERKELEY, *Italy in the Making, 1815–1848*, 3 Vols. Cambridge, 1932.

G. O. GRIFFITH, *Mazzini, Prophet of Modern Europe*, Hodder, 1932.

E. E. Y. HALES, *Mazzini and the Secret Societies*, Eyre & Spottiswoode, 1956.

E. E. Y. HALES, *Pio Nono*, Eyre & Spottiswoode, 1954.

D. MACK SMITH, *Italy*, Michigan Press, 1959.

J. A. R. MARRIOTT, *Makers of Modern Italy*, Oxford, 1931.

G. M. TREVELYAN, *Garibaldi's Defence of the Roman Republic*, Longmans, 1907. *Garibaldi and the Thousand*, Longmans, 1909.

C. J. S. SPRIGGE, *The Development of Modern Italy*, Duckworth, 1943.

A. J. WHYTE, *The Evolution of Modern Italy*, Blackwell, 1944.

18   Why was the Second Republic in France so short-lived?

French nineteenth-century politics can become extremely difficult to follow (much less understand) unless the student has a nodding acquaintance with some of the traditions and terms which recur time and again. Historians frequently refer to them with minimal explanation before plunging into further complexities of political analysis. At the risk, therefore, of insulting your intelligence, there follows a list of some of the terms and topics with which you ought to be conversant:

(i) What is meant by the use, in a political context, of the terms 'Right', 'Centre', and 'Left'.

What is meant, also, by the further sub-division of these groups.

The Right could be Legitimists, Orleanists, Bonapartists, Ultramontanes, upper-bourgeois followers of Guizot, etc., gradually shading into

The Centre, which could comprise constitutionalists, conservatives, moderates, liberals, the bourgeois generally, all with varying degrees of sympathy towards, alignment with, or hostility to

The Left, a generic term which might refer to any or all of republicans, radicals, socialists, revolutionaries, Jacobins, or just plain Reds.

(ii) The origins and development of the twin traditions of clericalism and anti-clericalism.

See how often questions like

the return of the Jesuits
Church control over education
re-endowment of the Church

crop up in the nineteenth century.

127

(iii) The 'Legend'—the Napoleonic Legend, the myth of the Liberal Empire and its misunderstood prophet, the fatal attraction of *La Gloire*—all assiduously cultivated by both bearers of the evocative name.

(iv) The great land settlement of the first Revolution, when all those Church estates changed hands. (Note how permanent such vast changes are. Consider the sweeping Saxon-Norman transference in the 1070s, or the quick sales of the vast monastic estates after 1536. The Saxons never got it back, and even a rabid catholic like Mary could not bully an otherwise compliant Parliament into re-endowing Mother Church.) So work out the attitude of this new class of land-owner in France to, say

> fresh revolutions
> government patronage of the Church
> land taxes.

What is likely to be their interest in distant political debates in Paris if their land settlement is not affected?

(v) The difference between Paris and the provinces.

The extent to which Paris dominated France.

> administration
> geography
> ideas
> communications (especially with the coming of the railways).

Therefore the extent to which the provinces always looked to Paris for a lead. (1789 is the exception.)

(vi) The perpetual bourgeois dilemma.

How to wring liberal concessions from a corrupt, oligarchic government without bringing the whole government down.

And if the government *has* fallen (as often as not due to spontaneous proletarian insurrection), how to prevent the 'people' sharing in the new political profits and privileges that are thus available.

(vii) The extent to which the Great Revolution dominated the imagination and behaviour of so many nineteenth-century would-be (and has-been) revolutionaries.

Was there perhaps too much artificial enthusiasm and self-conscious imitation of 1789 on the part of a vociferous, and misguided, minority? True, 1789 had turned the world upside-down, but you couldn't keep on turning the world upside-down.

Look at Guizot's comment on these people, at the end of the discussion of Question 19.

Now with this general knowledge at your disposal, see what relevant material can be drawn from an examination of the following:

(i) The revolution itself.

How many Frenchmen wanted it?
How many Frenchmen expected it?
How many Frenchmen knew what to do when it came?

(It seems to be one of the ironies of history that the ones taken most unawares by revolutions are often the very people who have spent years plotting them.)

(ii) The Provisional Government.

The political capacity of a man like Albert.

The staying power of political clubs and newspapers.

The voting figures for the first elections (on universal suffrage, note).

The weak points (from the republic's point of view) in the new constitution.

The public reaction to the 45 centimes tax.

(iii) The great opportunity for the romantics, the socialists, the theorists, the doctrinaires.
What happened to

Lamartine, the poet in politics.

Louis Blanc's much-publicised National Workshops.

Raspail's bid for the Presidency.

Barbès' and Blanqui's insurrection.

Proudhon's newspaper.

(iv) The behaviour of the Left.

How much unity of purpose and action was produced among its leaders?

How much agreement was there between the ideas of, say, Blanqui, Cabet, Blanc, Raspail, Ledru-Rollin?

How much political activity and support for Paris was there in the provinces?

To what extent did the radicals make a come-back in late 1849 and 1850?

What was the 'Red Scare', and how did it influence politics?

(v) The behaviour of the Centre.

The brief flirtation with the radicals until June, 1848.

The attempts to restrict the franchise.

The underestimation of Louis-Napoleon, especially by Thiers.

The Loi Falloux.

The overestimation of the radicals' strength.

(vi) The behaviour of the Right.

The attitude and activities of the Legitimists and Orleanists.

The cultivation of the Legend, and its effect on the Presidential election (a direct vote, remember).

The attempt to gain the support of Church and Army by means of the Roman expedition. (This did, however, backfire slightly. How?)

The new President's poor record prior to his election. Nearly everyone made the mistake of writing him off.

Louis-Napoleon's gift for theatricality.
  E.g. His countrywide tours and speeches.

    His pretended efforts to extend the (previously restricted) franchise.

    His timing of the coup for December 2nd, the anniversary of Austerlitz.

    The 'plebiscite' technique, so familiar to dictators. You provoke a crisis, swamp the electorate with propaganda, stiffen the police, and force a vote on the people, saying in effect, 'Choose: Me, or Anarchy.'

The planning of the coup.
How much of it was the work of Louis-Napoleon himself? And how accurate is it to attribute to him deep plots and dark ambitions long before December, 1851? Perhaps he belongs more to the tradition of opportunists like Bismarck and Hitler, who were all for giving the pot a stir, and seeing what tempting morsels came to the surface.

(vii) The economy.

    For example

    Were bread prices high or low?

    Had the population fully recovered from the great cholera epidemic?

    Were there any after-effects of the great railway boom and slump?

    How fast was the industrial revolution spreading, and where were its profits going?

(viii) Foreign relations.

    Were countries prepared to deal with the new regime?

    How many foreign governments even recognised the new republic?

    What would be the attitude of, say, the Tsar, or the Austrian Emperor?

    How would foreign liberals react to a regime which had put down a republic by force (Rome, 1849)?

Having collected your material, try to develop some theme. That does not mean that you must concoct one, and twist the facts to fit it. Rather, as you become acquainted with the topic, an idea, a train of thought, a line of development might occur to you. It gives the essay a spine. The examiner may not agree with you, but your essay will have the merit of shape; it will be saying something, putting forward a definite point of view.

For instance, what do you think of these ideas:

(i) The Second Republic was an unwanted foundling which nearly everyone hoped would die.
     The only ones who might have saved it, and who might have benefited from its survival—the radicals, the Left, or what you will—were too inexperienced to know how to keep it alive. It lost its life while its protectors squabbled among themselves over the best way to preserve it.

     So Louis-Napoleon merely buried something which was already dead.

(ii) The Second Republic was a healthy enough baby, tolerated, even liked by its bourgeois godparents, until it exhibited symptoms of the dread disease—mob rule. Terrified by the June Days, the bourgeois shrank away and sought refuge with the great protector of rights and property, the darling of the army, Louis-Napoleon. From there it was but a short step to the discreet suggestion that the stricken infant be put out of its misery for the good of all concerned.

     So Louis-Napoleon was cast in the role of hired assassin.

(iii) The Second Republic was the trusting innocent which placed itself under the protection of a scheming villain whose every thought was directed to its removal at the earliest possible opportunity.
      (There is evidence that the radical tradition in provincial France was stronger, and the opposition to the coup more widespread, than official Bonapartist propaganda cared to reveal.)

      So Louis-Napoleon's crime becomes cold-blooded, pre-meditated, inexcusable murder.

Reading list

D. W. BROGAN, *The French Nation, 1814–1940*, Hamilton, 1957.

J. P. T. BURY, *France, 1814–1940*, Methuen, 1969.

J. P. T. BURY, *Napoleon III and the Second Empire*, E.U.P., 1964.

A. COBBAN, *Pelican History of Modern France, Vol. II*, Pelican, 1965.

H. A. L. FISHER, *Bonapartism*, Oxford, 1957.

A. MAUROIS, *History of France*, Cape, 1960.

J. PLAMENATZ, *The Revolutionary Movement in France, 1815–1871*, Longmans, 1952.

R. POSTGATE, *The Story of a Year, 1848*, Cape, 1956.

F. SIMPSON, *The Rise of Louis-Napoleon*, Longmans, 1950.

J. M. THOMPSON, *Louis-Napoleon and the Second Empire*, Blackwell, 1954.

19 With what justification can nationalism be called the greatest single force at work in Europe in the first half of the 19th century?

Presumably with some, otherwise the idea would hardly have occurred to the examiners. So give the question the benefit of the doubt—to begin with at any rate.

Look for evidence of nationalism in the period prescribed.

But before you start it might be as well to sort out in your head a few ideas concerning the nature of nationalism itself.

For example, is it

the desire for political unity among all the people of a particular ethnic group.

the same desire among all those who speak the same language.

ditto among all those who merely happen to live in the same place. In other words, a purely geographical concept—a desire to tidy up the map.

the urge to expel an occupation force or minority government of a foreign power.

the urge to expel one's own government because it does not 'represent the nation'.

the compulsion to inflict one's own government, political doctrine, religious creed (or all three) on other 'nations'. In other words, does there have to be some element of aggression?

Now consider the following suggested examples of nationalism, and see if they fit into any (or none) of the foregoing categories. Perhaps there are other categories.

(i) The U S A   Not strictly speaking within the period prescribed by the question, but is it worthy of mention (by way of introduction) as having started it all? There might be a case for tracing both the national and the liberal traditions of the nineteenth century to Philadelphia and Yorktown.

(ii) The direct result of American inspiration.

> France, or rather the French Revolution. Are subsequent French conquests the first expression of a 'nation in arms'?

> In this context does England deserve consideration for her inspired, and often solitary, resistance to French aggression?

(iii) The 'self-defence' type.

> Spain (1808–14)
> Russia (1812)

> Question 4 offers comments on the extent to which this was the work of Spaniards and Russians.

> You might also consider how actively, consciously loyal the average peasant was to His Most Catholic Majesty or Our Holy Father the Tsar.

(iv) The 'self-determination' type.

> Serbia
> Greece
> Belgium
> Poland
> Hungary

Some names, dates, places and events will add bite to your argument.

What about Ireland?

Because there are two papers—on 'English' (which includes Ireland) and 'Foreign' History—there is often a tendency to departmentalise the mind, to neglect the obvious. 'Oh we've done English history; this is a "European" question.'

Well, at the risk of sounding banal, England (with Ireland), *is* part of Europe. Examples from its history often serve to illustrate an argument concerned with a 'European' question.

Lastly, in this connection, would it be cheating to include Spain's rebellious colonies in South America?

(v) The 'general overhaul' type.

> Was nationalism involved in any way with the attempts of some countries to put their house in order?

>> E.g. The efforts of Stein, Scharnhorst, and Gneisenau in Prussia.

>> The Sultan's spasmodic reforms in Turkey.

>> Mehemet Ali's schemes to modernise Egypt.

(vi) The 'consolidation' type.

> Italy
> Germany

>> These are the obvious examples. However, since the question said 'first half of the nineteenth century', it might be worth considering just how big, or successful, a force nationalism was in these two countries, *in the period under discussion*. Just because Italy and Germany were united in the end, it doesn't follow that they had every prospect of being united in 1830, or 1840 or 1850 (least of all perhaps in 1850). Cavour for example didn't expect to see Italian unity in his lifetime.

Well, there is some of the evidence at any rate for considering nationalism to be the 'greatest single force at work', as the question suggests. Now comes the time to challenge this suggestion.

And you really must 'think big'. This is a question of such enormous scope that you cannot afford to get enmeshed in details of marches and battles, protocols and treaties, pamphlets and speeches, technology and art, and so on. (Use details to illustrate your points, obviously, but the points come first. Detail is no good unless it is rationed and disciplined.)

The following list, of other 'forces at work' in the period under discussion, is intended simply to make you think. There is no question of any one of them being necessarily 'right', nor do they come in any order of merit or preference. Some you might accept as obvious; others you might consider because they hadn't occurred to you before; still others you might dismiss out of hand as so much nonsense.

After all, only *one* of them can be called 'the greatest single force at work in Europe in the first half of the nineteenth century'.

(i) Liberalism

Often inextricably involved with nationalism, especially in Germany, but there are still enough examples of liberal activity in the period to make a case for a separate liberal tradition.

E.g. France
Liberalism was largely what the French Revolution of 1789 was all about, wasn't it?

The other revolutions of 1830 and 1848.

England
The causes and effects of the Great Reform Act of 1832.

Naples (1820), Spain (1820), Modena (1831), Berlin and Prague (1848).

The Decembrists in Russia, the Burschenschaften in Germany, the Chartists in England, the 'banqueteers' in Paris, and so on, and so on.

(ii) Population

Most economic histories of Europe will provide figures for the huge rises in population.

Is therefore all this talk of nationalism and liberalism putting the cart before the horse? Was it all started by sheer numbers? Was it because there were simply so many people that

Nationalists talked so much about 'a people',
Liberals talked so much about 'the people'.

Does population density explain France's position in Europe at the beginning of the century in the same way as it explains Germany's at the end?

Does the rise in population provide the sole incentive for the great advances in agriculture and technology?

(iii) The Industrial/Agricultural Revolution.

Or is the boot on the other foot? Was it improvements in farming, medicine, and techniques of production which offered more material comfort, better health, greater security, and increased expectation of life?

And was it the sheer physical proximity of human beings in factories and cities which made the dissemination of political ideas so much easier?

(iv) Socialism

The intellectual child of industrialism, and concerned, unlike many liberals, with the lives of *all* the people.

Men like Babeuf, Owen, Saint-Simon, Fourier, Blanc, Proudhon, Engels, Marx—did they represent, or harness, or engender a great 'force' in European society?

(v) Catholicism

Just how big a recovery did the Church make after 1814? Assess the importance of factors like

the return of Jesuits.

the civil rights gained by Catholics in Britain.

the successes of the Ultra party in France.

the position of Metternich's Austria (the great Catholic champion) as arbiter of central Europe.

the fact that the Papacy was a serious candidate for leadership of a united Italy.

the pontificate of Pius IX, which saw, among other things, the promulgation of

the fully defined statement of the Immaculate Conception (1854).

the official claims of Papal infallibility (1870).

(vi) Absolutism

When all the dust had settled after the various liberal revolts (especially after 1848), just how many absolutist rulers had been turned (permanently) off their thrones? Perhaps there is a case for putting (v) and (vi) together and calling it something like the 'force of reaction'.

(vii) Internationalism

Did the early nineteenth century witness a major step towards mankind's political maturity in the shape of international partnership and regulation of human affairs?

E.g. The work of the Vienna Congress on international rivers and future conduct of international diplomacy.

The whole idea of the Congress system. (The word 'system' is used with reservations. See the discussion of it in Question 8.)

The Holy Alliance.

The attempts to get international condemnation of the slave trade.

(viii) Romanticism

The chemical reaction produced by the coincidence of the intellectual revolt against the rigid classicism and materialism of the late eighteenth century, the physical destruction of the society and politics of the *ancien régime,* and the unprecedented spread and interchange of ideas achieved by Napoleon's armies.

The new association of art and radical politics with bohemianism, poverty, evangelical fervour, utopianism, experimentation, and failure.

The omission of names is deliberate; if you mention one you must mention a hundred. The books will give ample examples from every sphere of human activity.

N.B. It is impossible to 'do' Romanticism in half a page. One can simply direct your attention to its existence, and give you a glimmering of its vastness and complexity.

(ix) Popular education

Examine the various educational reforms, especially of France and England.

Remember the colossal importance attached to education by the revived Catholic Church.

Trace the increased output of every type of cultural work from Carlyle's *History* and Scott's novels to the Grimms' *Fairy Tales* and the attempts to revive old languages like Erse, Flemish, Tuscan, Czech, and Provençal.

Does all this constitute a major step forward in what is arguably the greatest cause of all—the emancipation of the human mind?

(x) Determinism

Instead of the Aristotelian 'collection-of-information' approach typical of the eighteenth-century Encyclopaedists, the nineteenth century saw a more scientific, and at the same time more Platonic, speculative search for first principles, governing laws.

E.g. Bentham on society
Hegel on philosophy
Marx on politics and history
Darwin on biology.

All were trying to do for their branch of study what they thought Newton had done for physics.

(xi) The great 'divorce' of treason and heresy.

For centuries an inescapable fact of life had been that religious conformity and political obedience were inseparable. If you were a heretic, you were bound to be a traitor.

Did the nineteenth century see the start of the practical efforts to separate these two, to allow man the enjoyment of his private thoughts and beliefs? Had Voltaire and Tom Paine, for example, lived to 1850, would they have rejoiced at what they saw? Would Disraeli's career have been possible in the eighteenth century?

(xii) Steam

Since time immemorial the fastest means of travel had been the horse.

Consider

the commercial and industrial implications of steam power.

the political and military potential of railways.

the social effects of easy travel on people who had hitherto treated visitors from the next village as foreigners.

(xiii) 'Revolutionism', for want of a better word.

Did the French Revolution upset society so much that it became impossible to break the vicious circle of revolution/experiment/dissatisfaction/frustration/revolution?

Or, as Guizot put it, 'The French Revolution and the Emperor Napoleon I have thrown a certain number of minds, including some of the most distinguished, into a feverish excitement which becomes a moral and, I would almost say, a mental disease. They yearn for events, immense, sudden, and strange; they busy themselves with making and unmaking governments, nations, religions, society, Europe, the world . . . They are intoxicated with the greatness of their design, and blind to the chances of success. To hear them talk, one might think that they had the elements and ages at their command . . . and that these were the first days of creation or the last days of the world.'

There aren't any specific books which cover this question. Your answer should be a distillation of the knowledge gained from study of the various separate topics of the period.

However, the General List at the end might prove of some use.

20 'All the countries that participated in the Crimean War came to regret it sooner or later.' Discuss

The Crimean War is one of those topics which, for debatable reasons, lends itself to 'quotation questions'. You might equally well be asked to discuss any of the following:

'The Crimean War was a war without a decision.'

'The Crimean War destroyed the Concert of Europe.'

'The Crimean War was the original bad joke of history.'

'The last thing the Crimean War was "about" was the Crimea.'

'The Crimean War was a nineteenth-century war fought by eighteenth-century men and methods.'

'The Crimean War was a war none of its participants wanted to fight.'

In each case you draw on the same body of knowledge. A rough outline of this body of knowledge is as follows:

(i) The setting

Another chapter in the long feud between Russia and Turkey. Wars had been fought pretty regularly since 1768. That one finished in 1774. Others were 1787–92, 1806–12, 1828–29.

Another chapter in the Eastern Question generally, following in the tradition of Catherine the Great's Greek Project, Serbian and Greek independence, the campaigns of Ibrahim, the Treaty of Unkiar Skelessi, and the revolt of Mehemet Ali.

Another move to prevent Russia upsetting the Balance of Power, a fearsome prospect which had given nightmares to Western statesmen since Alexander had negotiated 'sword in hand' at Vienna—doubly fearsome now that Nicholas had emerged from the holocaust of 1848–49 as the saviour of the Hapsburgs, and the only monarch (besides Victoria) who could proclaim his country's immunity to revolution.

142

(ii) Causes and pretexts

The 'sick man of Europe' controversy, and the views of Nicholas, Aberdeen, and Palmerston.

The Danubian Principalities (Moldavia and Wallachia), and their relevance to
>   Austrian trade-routes.
>   Turkish territorial integrity.
>   Russian expansionism.
>   Balkan nationalism.

The neutrality of the Black Sea.

The Holy Places.

Guardianship of Orthodox Christian subjects of the Sultan.

The ambitions of Louis Napoleon

>   to bring the 'Legend' to life.

>   to champion the cause of nationalism, and of the Catholic Church.

>   to wrest the political initiative in Europe from the reactionary powers.

The ideological issue

>   West v. East.

>   liberalism v. reaction.

>   the champions of 'justice' and 'freedom' v. the 'gendarme of Europe'.

The tremendous force of ill-informed, but vociferous, public opinion, especially in England.

The worsening of Austro-Russian relations.

The Vienna Note.

Menschikov's visit to Constantinople.

The extent of the influence of Stratford de Redcliffe on the Sultan.

The Russian invasion of the Principalities (July, 1853), and the naval victory over the Turks at Sinope (November, 1853).

(iii) Campaigns

The Baltic

The Arctic

Kamchatka

The Caucasus

The Crimea.

(iv) The participants

The Russians, obviously.

The Turks, equally obviously.

The Allies, the French and English. How would they overcome problems like

getting there.
staying there (supplies, etc.).
unity of command, between two nations which, from 1346 to 1815, had been 'natural enemies'.

The Sardinians.
What on earth were they doing there?
Who invited them?
How well did they acquit themselves?

(v) The non-participants

Prussia (What was her interest in the Eastern Question?)

Austria

Russia's traditional partners in reaction.
Something must have gone seriously wrong with Russian foreign policy if they could no longer

command the allegiance of Austria and Prussia against the 'revolution'.

keep France in check by the double threat of

Prussian activity on the Rhine.
Austrian advances in Italy.

Examine the Hapsburg dilemma

Temperament should have aligned them with Russia, but Russian success would have given the Tsar the mouth of the Danube.

Expediency (the shoring up of Turkey against Russia) might have pushed Austria towards the Allies, but Russian defeat would have made Louis Napoleon the arbiter of Europe, and open up no end of troublesome prospects concerned with Italian and Balkan nationalism.

(vi) The Peace of Paris, 1856

Examine the scope and practicality of its terms.

What significance is there in the fact that it was signed in Paris?

Just what did Cavour get out of his admission to the peace conference?

(vii) The effects of the war

Louis Napoleon's enhanced prestige.

The humbling (temporary at any rate) of Russia.

The domestic reforms thrust upon governments by the war.

E.g. Military overhaul in Britain.

The achievements in medical reform of Florence Nightingale in England, and Pirogov and the Grand Duchess Elena Pavlovna in Russia.

What connection is there between Alexander II's defeat in 1856 and his emancipation of the serfs in 1861?

The continuance (however gradual) of the fragmentation of the Ottoman Empire.

The setting up of Rumania.

The break-up of the Holy Alliance.

The thrusting of Austria into the diplomatic wilderness. How strong a line of cause and effect is there between Austria's fatal hesitation in 1853 and

>her defeat in 1859
>the destruction at Sadowa
>the Compromise of 1867?

Then there are the verdicts on the Crimean War, which have their usual share of glibness, bias, and objective truth.

E.g.

1. The Crimean War was the first war in which the telegraph, war correspondents, and public opinion played a large part.

2. It was the last war for a long time to produce any international conference to settle the outstanding differences. Its immediate successors

>the Italian War of Liberation, 1859
>the American Civil War, 1861–65
>the Austro-Prussian War, 1866
>the Franco-Prussian War, 1870–71

were more conclusive affairs in which the victor imposed terms.

3. Coming midway between the last great eighteenth-century war (1815) and the first total war (1914–18), it had, in almost comic juxtaposition, elements of both.

E.g.

The Allied expectation that the Russian army would obligingly wait in Rumania for their army to come and defeat it (Gilbertian farce), and the sordid reality of the final casualty list of over half a million, two-thirds of it due to pneumonia, typhus, cholera, and gangrene.

The appearance of the first warships driven by steam, in collaboration with an army that was housed in tents first purchased for use in the Peninsular War.

The hiring of navvies for the construction of a railway to supply an army whose commander-in-chief (Raglan) referred to the enemy from force of habit as 'the French'.

4. The Crimean War was not about the Crimea any more than

the 1914 War was about Belgium.

the American Civil War was about Fort Sumter.

the Second Punic War was about Saguntum.

Your task now resolves itself into shaping as much of this evidence as possible to fit the wording of the question. This does not mean falsifying evidence, or twisting arguments; it is rather a matter of phraseology and presentation.

For instance,

(i) On the face of it, the causes of the war would appear to be irrelevant, since you are being asked about the participants' feelings once they've joined in.

But if you start from the point that the belligerents (except France possibly) regretted the war even breaking out—a perfectly legitimate opening for the discussion—you can then use your knowledge of the causes and pretexts to show how the game of diplomatic bluff and counter-bluff, the false assumptions and wrong interpretations, led inexorably to a war, a war everyone felt sucked into in order to maintain prestige.

(ii) Again, on the face of it, any mention of Austria is out because she was not a participant. But there is a great deal of material on Austria which is worth saying if only it can be made to fit. So how about something like

'The countries that participated in the Crimean War had some causes for regret because of so-and-so, but also had considerable cause for satisfaction because of so-and-so. The irony really lies elsewhere. The country which had most regrets concerning the war—which didn't even want the war fought at all—was the country which didn't fight—Austria, because . . . ' and away you go.

This way you are not merely showing off that you happen to know about Austria; you are volunteering extra information which is still being kept subservient to the overall argument.

The trick is to get as much as possible across to the examiner without being too obvious about it; to be discursive and informative at the same time; to give the impression that, for his benefit, you are sharing your knowledge, not airing it.

Reading list

M. S. ANDERSON, *The Eastern Question*, Macmillan, 1966.
J. P. T. BURY, *Napoleon III and the Second Empire*, E.U.P., 1964.
C. HIBBERT, *The Destruction of Lord Raglan*, Pelican, 1969.
B. LEWIS, *The Emergence of Modern Turkey*, Oxford, 1968.
J. A. R. MARRIOTT, *The Eastern Question*, Oxford, 1940.
W. MILLER, *The Ottoman Empire and its Successors, 1801–1927*, Cass, 1966.
B. PARES, *A History of Russia*, Cape, 1955.
W. PEMBERTON, *Battles of the Crimea*, Batsford, 1962.
H. SETON-WATSON, *The Russian Empire, 1801–1917*, Oxford, 1967.
R. W. SETON-WATSON, *England and Europe, 1789–1914*, Cambridge, 1937.
F. A. SIMPSON, *Louis Napoleon and the Recovery of France*, Longmans, 1951.
A. J. P. TAYLOR, *The Struggle for Mastery in Europe, 1848–1918*, Oxford, 1954.
A. J. WHYTE, *The Political Life and Letters of Cavour, 1848–1861*, Oxford, 1930.
C. WOODHAM-SMITH, *Florence Nightingale*, Fontana, 1968.
C. WOODHAM-SMITH, *The Reason Why*, Constable, 1953, Penguin, 1968.

21 Why was it that Mazzini failed, and Cavour succeeded, in uniting Italy?

When lawyers ask a question, they want it to be answered—nothing more, nothing less. When history examiners set a question, they expect it to be answered, but they would like it to be pulled to pieces first. To put it another way, the one is intended simply to elicit information; the other is designed to stimulate thought.

So it is often a good idea, before you go about writing an answer, to 'question the question'. Is it logical? Is it fair? What sort of information is it after? Above all, what assumptions and implications does it make by its very wording?

This one, for instance, is, on the face of it, asking for two lists of reasons, which the obedient candidate, with his 'Key Facts' drummed into his weary memory, obligingly scribbles down in breathless (rather than deathless) prose before he forgets them.

Now have a good look at the wording. It bristles with all sorts of assumptions and implications.

E.g. (i) that Mazzini failed.

     (ii) that Cavour succeeded.

     (iii) that the one is somehow opposite to, or complementary to, the other.

     (iv) that Italian unification was straightforward, complete, or desirable.

     (v) that no other agency had anything to do with Italian unification.

Consider them.

     (i) Mazzini's failure.

         Examine Mazzini's career

            his membership of the Carbonari

            his essays in politics in Piedmont

            his exile

his 'Young Italy' movement

his republicanism

his burning belief in the unity of all Italy—'Never rise in any other name than of Italy and of all Italy'

his low opinion of Cavour

his attempts at the government of Rome

the effects on the Italian mind of his passionate writings

his doctrine of the Third Rome

his firm conviction that the expulsion of the Austrians came before all else.

Did all this amount to nothing but utter failure? Was there no contribution at all to the cause of Italian unity?

Do not forget that voices crying in the wilderness may move empires even though the owner of the voice may have a thin time himself out there amid the locusts and wild honey.

(ii) Cavour's success.

Find out what you can about

Cavour's early career, his stay in England, his early portfolios in Piedmont, etc.

his personal abilities.

the lessons he learnt from the failures of 1848–9.

his decision to join the Crimean War.

his membership of the Peace Congress at Paris in 1856.

the plotting with Louis Napoleon.

the business of the Austrian ultimatum.

his conduct before and after Villafranca.

his subsequent handling of Louis Napoleon and Garibaldi.

his share in the creation of the northern Kingdom and in the later union with the central states.

the affair of the Two Sicilies.

his views on Italian nationalism and liberalism.

How much of Italy was united when Cavour died?

(iii) The connection between Mazzini's failure and Cavour's success.

Was it simply a case of Cavour doing right all the things Mazzini had done wrong?

Was it necessary for Mazzini's republicanism to fail before Cavour's monarchical method could succeed?

Who was the greater statesman: Mazzini with his plots and stillborn republics, or Cavour with his cynical diplomacy and manipulation of European opinion?

Who was the greater patriot: Mazzini with his blazing faith in the destiny of 'all Italy', or Cavour with his creed of the gradual absorption (as occasion permitted) of the peninsula by the Piedmontese Crown?

(iv) The straightforwardness, completeness, or desirability of Italian unity.

1. Straightforwardness

Consider the variety of views on the means of uniting Italy. (See the remarks in the section on Italian nationalism in the first half of the nineteenth century.)

Estimate the opposition the Piedmontese monarchy met in its progress towards hegemony in Italy.

2. Completeness

Decide what the scope of the essay is going to be.

If you intend to restrict it to the careers of Mazzini and Cavour, then clearly Italy was not united.

If you interpret it as a discussion on Italian unity, then you can look back to the glimpses of unity given by Napoleonic administration, and look ahead to the absorption of Venetia and Rome.

3. Desirability

Examine the views of the interested parties. Just who wanted Italy united?

Mazzini did, and Garibaldi.

Austria didn't, obviously.

The Prussians and the Russians were not well disposed towards such popular movements except in so far as they embarrassed Austria.

Cavour himself didn't want or expect unity, certainly not in 1859, anyway.

Louis Napoleon, for all his fine sentiments, wanted a grateful set of satellite states, not a strong monarchy beyond the Alps. (In that sense he fitted into the tradition of all French adventurers in Italy from Charlemagne and Charles VIII to Napoleon I.)

Ironically, the only great power to express itself in favour, Britain, was the one country which took no active steps to further it.

(v) The implied absence of other agencies working for Italian unity. How much importance should be attached to factors like

Austria's diplomatic isolation after 1856.

Louis Napoleon's military assistance, at Magenta and Solferino.

Garibaldi (both military and publicity value).

Victor Emmanuel, from his first defiance of the Austrians in 1849, to his entry into Rome in 1871.

Lord John Russell's negative assistance, and the overwhelming moral approval of English public opinion.

the embarrassment and defeat of Austria by Prussia in 1866.

the defeat of France in 1870–71.

Do not neglect opportunities to offer comparisons with, to make references to, other countries or other periods in order to make a particular point more telling or vivid. It adds to the essay's fluency, and shows that you are not merely concerned, like the obedient candidate mentioned above, to pour as many 'Key facts' on to the page as possible.

For example

Compare Mazzini with other men of letters who made forays into practical politics, like Petofi, Lamartine, Cobbett.

Draw some valid parallels between Italian and German unification.

Make the obvious comparison between Cavour and Bismarck.

Offer a (less obvious?) comparison between Cavour and Lincoln, who died in the hour of victory.

Reading list

H. ACTON, *The Bourbons of Naples*, Methuen, 1956.

R. ALBRECHT-CARRIÉ, *Italy, from Napoleon to Mussolini*, Columbia, 1960.

G. O. GRIFFITH, *Mazzini, Prophet of Modern Europe*, Hodder, 1932.

E. E. Y. HALES, *Mazzini and the Secret Societies*, Eyre & Spottis-woode, 1956.

D. MACK SMITH, *Italy*, Michigan Press, 1959.

J. A. R. MARRIOTT, *Makers of Modern Italy*, Oxford, 1931.

C. J. S. SPRIGGE, *The Development of Modern Italy*, Duckworth, 1943.

A. J. P. TAYLOR, *The Struggle for Mastery in Europe, 1848–1918*, Oxford, 1954.

G. M. TREVELYAN, *Garibaldi and the Making of Italy*, Longmans, 1911.

A. J. WHYTE, *The Evolution of Modern Italy*, Blackwell, 1944.

A. J. WHYTE, *The Political Life and Letters of Cavour, 1848–61*, Oxford, 1930.

22 To what extent did the Napoleonic Legend affect the foreign policy of the Second Empire?

Possible introductions:

   (i) The growth of the 'Legend' after 1815, or rather after 1821.

       E.g. the histories
           the war memoirs
           the pink mist of fond memory
           the splendid tomb at Les Invalides
           the Arc de Triomphe.

  (ii) A comparison between Napoleon I and Napoleon III, to show that sequels, however self-consciously imitative, very rarely come up to the standard of the original version.

 (iii) Louis Napoleon's *coup d'état.*

      He had declared himself Emperor; it followed that he had to have an empire to rule over.

      Moreover, he was the newcomer among European rulers; he had to prove himself by doing more than having international exhibitions at Paris.

You need to have some idea of what the Napoleonic Legend meant. What were the pressures that it exerted on Louis Napoleon and his fellow-countrymen?

 1. The role of France as the guardian of the revolutionary principle of 'Liberty'.

      At home it could lead to Louis Napoleon's experiments towards genuine parliamentary rule, the Liberal Empire.

      Abroad, it could be used by an unscrupulous ruler to justify all sorts of interference in the politics of other countries. Its sacred text was probably the Declaration of Fraternity of November, 1792.

 2. French leadership in Europe—if not overlordship, at least predominance, a control of the political initiative.

3. French destiny as conqueror of Italy.

Incidentally, it went back far beyond the time of Napoleon I—as far as Charles VIII at the end of the fifteenth century, arguably as far as Charlemagne.

4. More vaguely, but more simply, the Past, which bewitched millions of Frenchmen, and not only unemployed army officers on half-pay.

Many reflected that other regimes

Bourbon misrule, before 1789 and after 1815
Orleanist constitutional monarchy (a king with an umbrella!)
Republican bickerings of Jacobins in the 1790's,
and Socialists in the 1840's

had brought France singularly little dignity, or prestige.

Under the Empire, France mattered.
Louis Napoleon had a vast fund of unconscious goodwill to draw upon, initially at any rate.

5. The Napoleonic belief in destiny (an idea recently at work, they say, in the unfathomable mind of General de Gaulle).

Napoleon was the child of the Revolution.

Louis Napoleon believed he was the man of the hour.

Like so many public figures who concocted a public character for themselves, he became to some extent taken in by his own propaganda, and, later, was forced to act, because of the Legend, in a manner contrary to his inclinations, and over and above his true capabilities.

It was easy for him to gird on the Emperor's sword; he looked a fine figure. It was a different matter when he felt himself bound to wield it.

Now collect information on the following issues, and decide how the influence of the Legend made itself felt in the way Louis Napoleon faced them.

Of course the question did specify the 'foreign policy of the Second Empire', which need not necessarily mean the same thing as the 'foreign policy of Louis Napoleon'. His conspiratorial character tended to take him behind his ministers' backs on occasions.

If you can find sufficiently detailed material to make this difference clear, so much the better. But it would be reasonable to assume that the question was asking you what you know about Louis Napoleon.

1. Getting accepted. Persuading Europe to recognise the *coup d'état* in the first place.

   After all, what promise of permanence could he offer, having just overthrown a republic which, as its first president, he had sworn a solemn oath to preserve?

   And his career before that had been pretty undistinguished, to say the least.

2. The Crimean War. Remember France's comparatively poor showing in the Near East between 1798 and 1841.

3. The Peace Conference at Paris. (Note too France's attitude towards the proposed union of Moldavia and Wallachia.)

4. Italy. Plombières and Villafranca.

   Savoy and Nice (France's first territorial gains since Vienna).

5. Algeria, Senegal, Dakar.

   Strictly speaking 'colonial' rather than 'foreign', but arguably relevant inasmuch as France's moves in these directions might concern other powers with colonial ambitions.

6. The Anglo-French expedition to Pekin.

7. The French expedition to Syria.

8. The Cobden Free Trade Treaty.

9. The Polish insurrection.

10. The Schleswig-Holstein question.

11. The Austro-Prussian struggle for German leadership.

12. The Mexican enterprise.

13. The Spanish Crown question.

14. The Franco-Prussian War.

If you have explained the effect of the Legend on France's attitude to the above issues, you have produced an answer to the question, but not necessarily a complete answer.

Remember, it said 'To what extent'.

Suppose you have replied, in effect, 'The Legend affected French foreign policy only about 60 per cent.' The other 40 per cent needs explaining. The question is about the Legend, true, and the Legend therefore commands attention, and detailed examination. But the balance must be kept. Other factors must be mentioned (the 40 per cent), however briefly, if only to show that you are aware of the full picture.

Even if every statement you made about the Legend was fair, balanced, and true, the answer would not be complete if you left it at that. The picture could be grossly out of focus.

And supposing you have come to the conclusion that the Legend was only 30–40 per cent responsible for Louis Napoleon's behaviour. If you failed to mention anything else, the picture you would present, despite its truthfulness, would be as deceptive as a pack of lies.

Well, then, having laboured the point so much, what were these 'other factors'?

That's just it—with Louis Napoleon, you're never sure.

1. Was it his character?—a bit seedy.

> Possessed of much of his uncle's realism, but lacking that final touch of callousness to pursue something to the bitter end.

> What A. J. P. Taylor called 'a procrastinating adventurer'. (Work that one out!)

> A mixture of Don Quixote and Machiavelli, with a touch of Hamlet thrown in (and that one!).

2. Was it his early life?—Exile, prison, plots, and so on.

> It is said of him that he never lost his taste for conspiracy. (Cavour pandered to this at Plombières.)

3. Was it his self-conscious role as champion of European nationalities?

   Does this explain his behaviour over the questions of
                    Poland?
                    Rumania?
                    Italy?

4. Was it the typical dictator's trick of pursuing a vigorous foreign
   policy in order to distract attention from oppressive or unsuccessful government at home?

5. Was it his desire to conciliate the strong body of Catholic
   opinion?

   Even while President of the pathetic Second Republic, he had
   launched the army against the Roman insurgents in order to
   restore the Pope.

6. Was it his eagerness to please the Army?

   After all, he was a Bonaparte. (Or perhaps this is part of the
                    Legend?)

7. Was it the maintenance of the good relations between France and
   England which Guizot had laboured to build?

In fact, looking at the above list, is it reasonable to argue that this
whole business of the Legend was a bit overdone?
   Does it not take a real Napoleon to pursue a Napoleonic foreign
policy?

Reading list

D. W. BROGAN, *The French Nation, 1814–1940*, Hamilton, 1957.

J. P. T. BURY, *France, 1814–1940*, Methuen, 1969.

J. P. T. BURY, *Louis Napoleon and the Second Empire*, E.U.P., 1964.

A. COBBAN, *A History of Modern France*, Vol. II., Pelican, 1965.

H. A. L. FISHER, *Bonapartism*, Oxford, 1957.

P. GUEDALLA, *The Second Empire*, Hodder, 1946.

J. H. JACKSON (Ed.), *A Short History of France*, Cambridge, 1959.

F. A. SIMPSON, *The Rise of Louis Napoleon*, Longmans, 1950.

F. A. SIMPSON, *Louis Napoleon and the Recovery of France*, Longmans, 1951.

A. J. P. TAYLOR, *The Struggle for Mastery in Europe, 1848–1918*, Oxford, 1954.

J. M. THOMPSON, *Louis Napoleon and the Second Empire*, Blackwell, 1954.

T. ZELDIN, *Napoleon III*, History Today, February, 1958.

T. ZELDIN, *The Political System of Napoleon III*, Macmillan, 1958.

23   Examine the part played by Prussia in German affairs, 1840–71

Never assume, because a couple of dates are used to fix (artificial) limits to the scope of a question, that there is necessarily anything special about them. It may well be that, for convenience, the examiners have chosen years in which, say, a treaty was signed, or a battle fought, or a new boundary fixed. In this case, presumably, because Frederick William III died in 1840 and the German Empire was declared in the Hall of Mirrors at Versailles in 1871. In that sense, yes, they are special.

But they are not necessarily special in starting things or finishing things. To put it another way, this question is, roughly, about Prussia's rise to leadership in and over Germany. But it doesn't follow that 1840 caused, or marked, the beginning of this rise, or that 1871 caused or marked the end of it. (For instance it could well be that the growth of Prussian industrialism or the workings of the Federal Constitution tightened still further Prussia's control over Germany.) And while we're about it, it doesn't follow either because Prussia was a second-rank power in 1840 and a first-rank power in 1871, that her rise was constant or unchecked.

Remember always that dates like this are merely terms of convenience. To give another example, one has to call the period from 1800 to 1899 something, so historians employ the term 'nineteenth century'. But there wouldn't be much difference felt by contemporaries between December, 1799 and January, 1800. Indeed, many historians argue that the eighteenth century really ended in 1789 (the Bastille) or 1799 (Brumaire) or 1815 (Waterloo).

And think of the various dates suggested to mark the 'end' of the Middle Ages:

E.g.

1452 Birth of Leonardo.

1485 Battle of Bosworth (a very insular view).

1487 Rounding of the Cape by Diaz.

161

1492 Discovery of America by Columbus.

1517 Luther's protest against Rome.

1536 Dissolution of the monasteries (another insular view).

16th century   The development and use of the printing press, or gunpowder, or the mariner's compass, or the heliocentric theory of the solar system, etc.

Late 17th century   The Scientific Revolution.

All these dates, and the two in question, are merely convenient chronological vantage points. By virtue of this fact, you are provided with a ready means of opening and closing the essay:

1. By showing to what extent the processes of Prussia's rise to power were evident before 1840.

2. By pointing out that Prussia did not necessarily stop rising after 1871.

To digress just a little more before discussing the question, you may consider this attempt to minimise the importance of a single event or a single year unfair, even misinformed. You may be of the opinion that certain events, or the events of a certain year, have a unique, shattering, and permanent effect upon the history of a race or a country or an institution.

You should be aware, however, that there are always these two views of history:

1. That historical change is wrought by the steady and gradual interaction of a variety of factors.

2. That the course of history can be radically and permanently altered by single events, which owe nothing to the past.

Call them if you like the 'continuity' view and the 'cataclysmic' view of history.

Take two examples with many parallels to each other—the French Revolution and the Russian Revolution. It was fashionable for the apologists of the Jacobins and the Soviets to regard all history pre-1789 and pre-1917 as 'wrong' and therefore valueless; to claim that, because the revolutions contradicted and defeated their predecessors they therefore derived nothing *from* their predecessors. The revolutions were unique cataclysms.

When the dust had settled, along came a generation of continuity historians to discover and point out that the revolutionaries on the contrary owed a great deal to their predecessors, and that things hadn't really changed all that much:

E.g.

Anticlericalism in France went back long before 1789.

The French taste for omnicompetent executives derived not from Napoleon but from Richelieu and Louis XIV.

The Russians' acceptance of Soviet dictatorship was to be explained not by belief in Marxist dogma but by the ingrained habit of obedience to centuries of Tsarist absolutism.

There is also, sooner or later, a third group of historians who examine *everything* and say in effect, 'of course it was really six of one and half a dozen of the other'. They are detailed, and fair, and balanced, and scrupulous. But they are usually not half as interesting and stimulating as the first two.

Well, now, Prussia, between 1840 and 1871. Collect information on the following:

1. The part Prussia was already playing in 1840:

   E.g. The effect in Germany of Prussia's tremendous overhaul of every department of government.

   The results for German economy and society of the new decrees allowing free economic activity for Jews, and free occupational choice for everybody.

   The impact on German thought of the University of Berlin.

   The founding of the Zollverein.

   The beginning of a railway network.

   The already advanced 'Prussianisation' of Silesia, West Prussia, and Rhineland Prussia.

2. Frederick William IV, the new king in 1840, and, later, his successor, William I, who subsequently became German Emperor.

3. Prussia's relations with, and attitude to, Metternich and the Bund.

4. The growth of the Zollverein after 1840.

5. Prussia and the revolutions of 1848:

> E.g. Did this make or break any alliance between Prussia and German liberals?
>
> Did Prussia really lose an opportunity to seize the leadership of a united Germany?

6. The Erfurt Union, and the subsequent humiliation at Olmütz by Schwarzenberg.

7. The Crimean War—did the status of Prussia and Austria as non-combatants have any effect on their position in Germany or their relations with each other?

8. Did Prussia benefit from Austria's defeat in the Italian War of 1859?

9. Schleswig-Holstein—a problem which involved Prussia and Austria, and which continued, on and off, from 1839 to 1865.

10. The war with Austria, 1866. How far was Prussia's victory responsible for the *Ausgleich* of 1867?

11. The North German Confederation, 1867.

12. 1870–71—the war against France, and the creation of the German Empire.

13. The importance of the Prussian army, and the contributions of Gneisenau, Scharnhorst, Clausewitz, von Roon and von Moltke.

14. The silent conquest of Germany that was going on all the time:

> E.g. The growth, spread, and efficiency of the Prussian civil service.
>
> The steadily increasing wealth and power of the Zollverein.
>
> It was railways which made Prussian troops so mobile in 1866.

The effect on the German mind of Berlin University and
its luminaries

>Ranke
>Humboldt
>Grimm
>Ritter
>Mommsen
>Hegel

15. Bismarck—how much credit for Prussia's success is due to him?

As always, try and develop a theme, and group your material in
such a way that it illustrates and explains this theme:

E.g.

(i) The gradual but relentless destruction of the Hapsburg legend.

(ii) The eclipse of German liberalism by German, or rather
Prussian, nationalism.

(iii) Prussian fortunes plunge to their nadir in 1850–51, and then
soar to unique heights in the 1860's.

(iv) It was not politics (or blood, or iron, or Bismarck) which
placed Prussia at the head of Germany, but economics.
Rather a coincidence that Marx should have published *Das
Kapital* in 1867, or that Darwin proclaimed the 'survival of
the fittest' in 1859.

Beware the usual misconceptions that:

Prussia was the 'obvious' candidate for German leadership.

Germany was 'united'.

Bismarck 'saw through' Louis Napoleon.

the Prussian army had an unbroken tradition of invincibility
stretching from Rossbach to Sedan.

Bismarck had a blueprint for the 'unification' of Germany
drawn up as soon as he became Chancellor.

Finally, what did the part played by Prussia in German affairs amount to? The following conjectures are offered as statements for simplicity's sake.

(i) It produced the triumph of nationalism at the expense of liberalism.

(ii) It killed the Second Empire in France. This, and the filling of the power vacuum in the middle of the great North European Plain, drastically altered the Balance of Power in Europe.

(iii) Germany was conquered, not united. Austria's exclusion meant, if anything, disunity.

(iv) Austria was forced out of Germany, and therefore South-Eastwards, ultimately to seek a reckoning with her rival for Balkan hegemony, Russia. It is an irony (or poetic justice?) that the man responsible for this defeat and expulsion, Bismarck, should have spent so many sleepless nights worrying how to prevent the logical outcome of his handiwork, a war between Austria and Russia. 1914 was to prove that he, like Metternich, understood that the real enemy of European monarchy was not the 'revolution', but war.

(v) Prussia drilled into the German brain the doctrine of the Sovereign State, and generations of Berlin University historians reiterated the myth of Prussia's mission to unite Germany, until even the Germans believed it.

There is an interesting contrast between Prussia and England, later to be such bitter enemies.

Under the supreme sovereignty of the State, the Prussians spent their lives in worship of the Trinity of Authority, Industry (in both senses), and Efficiency. Their approach was always that of the professional.

At the same time, the English, under the Reign of Law, were forging their great new educational trivium of Classics, Cricket, and Christianity (in that order), and they took pride in an approach that was defiantly amateur.

While the Prussian bureaucrats sucked their pens and absorbed Germany, English officers and gentlemen showed the natives how they ought to run their lives.

Which was the greater error—the Prussian mission to unite Germany, or the British mission to civilise the world?

Reading list

R. FLENLEY, *Modern German History*, Dent, 1968.

W. O. HENDERSON, *The Zollverein*, Cass, 1968.

J. A. R. MARRIOTT and C. G. ROBERTSON, *The Evolution of Modern Prussia*, Oxford, 1946.

W. MEDLICOTT, *Bismarck*, E.U.P., 1965.

E. J. PASSANT, *A Short History of Germany, 1815–1945*, Cambridge, 1959.

C. G. ROBERTSON, *Bismarck*, Constable, 1918.

A. J. P. TAYLOR, *Bismarck, the Man and the Statesman*, Hamilton, 1955.

A. J. P. TAYLOR, *The Course of German History since 1815*, Hamilton, 1948.

A. J. P. TAYLOR, *The Struggle for Mastery in Europe, 1848–1918*, Oxford, 1954.

24   Why was Spain no longer a great power during this period?

A big question, this—in the sense that 1789–1871 is a long time to condense into a single essay, even when only one country is concerned. And if you decide, as is more than likely, that Spain had ceased to be a great power long before 1789, the question becomes even bigger.

Two problems then present themselves:

(i) The difficulty of preventing the essay becoming too detailed, too much a recital of events.

(ii) The difficulty of knowing how to cover each of the separate aspects of the subject.

You have to learn, from bitter experience, how to be aware of what you're writing. For example,

have you put in too many details of military engagements?

have you neglected the economic factors?

have you devoted three-quarters of the essay to a discussion of the events of a single decade? (If so, how would you justify it?)

In a sense, you have to split your mind in two, one half busily writing and concentrating on scholarship, the other half standing over the first and supervising, checking, correcting the structure of the essay.

A very useful rule of thumb is to keep a sort of reference list of various factors which influence historical development. Look to see whether your essay has in fact offered reasons, comments, explanations, etc., under the separate headings.

For example, is it altogether too fanciful to suppose that the following seven factors

political	social
economic	geographical
fortuitous	religious
personal	

constitute the seven colours of the historical prism, which, when fused, produce the white light of truth?

You can probably think of other factors just as important, maybe more so. You may wish to extend the list of seven, or to cut it, or to change it beyond recognition. But it is still useful to have a formula *like* this at your disposal to help you review your material, to enable you to spot the gaps in your knowledge. One of the first steps to learning, we are told, is to find out just how ignorant we are.

For the sake of argument, apply this list to Spanish history, and see just how varied and valid is the material you come up with.

N.B. As is customary in this book, the following suggestions are put forward in the shape of factual statements, in order to avoid plastering the page with question-marks. Always remember that they are suggestions, and in many cases also generalisations, and are to be treated as such.

1. Political

> Spain was constantly prey to factional dispute, military revolution, and civil war, any or all of which could give easy opportunity for foreign intervention. The pattern went back as far as the Moorish invasion of the 8th century, when disputes among Visigothic princes gave the sons of the Prophet their chance. Further examples could be found from almost every century of Spanish history:
>
> | | |
> |---|---|
> | 14th | the intrigues and campaigns of du Guesclin and the Black Prince. John of Gaunt even claimed the Castilian throne. |
> | 18th | the war of the Spanish Succession. |
> | 19th | the intervention of France after the 1820 revolt against Ferdinand. |
>
> So much of Spain's energy was diverted by her rulers (many of them not Spanish) away from her true interests:
>
> North Africa
> Sicily and Asia Minor
> the Low Countries
> the New World.
>
> There was a strong tradition of regional loyalties which constantly bedevilled any attempts at creating effective centralised government:
>
> Aragonese
> Valencian
> Catalan
> and of course the Basques.

2. Social

>The unproductive classes (from the nobility and the upper clergy to vagrant schoolmasters and redundant monks) were far too numerous and far too difficult to remove.

>The middle classes were either too weak or too divided:

>>physically, spread thin around coastal cities.
>>emotionally, due to regional loyalties.

3. Economic

>The colossal output of bullion from Spain's American Empire did anything but make Spain wealthy:

>>it inflated prices.

>>it discouraged the spirit of industry.

>>it was diverted to pay for costly and unproductive European wars.

>Spain did not derive the fullest benefits from her empire anyway:

>>her navy couldn't control it.

>>she did not produce enough cheap manufactured goods to supply it.

>Because of these, and because of an outworn mercantilist code, the colonies sought satisfaction with Spain's rivals/enemies. 'Spain kept the cow, the rest of Europe drank the milk.'

>Within Spain, transport costs remained high:

>>long mountain ranges.
>>bad roads.
>>the late arrival of railways.

>Only the coastal areas enjoyed cheap sea transport.

The savage persecution of Jews and Moriscos did as much harm to the Spanish economy as the hounding of the Huguenots did to the French.

4. Geographical

The great variety of topography and climate favoured regionalism.

It also made nation-wide legislation extremely difficult, especially before modern means of communication facilitated the collection of reliable information.

The terrible dryness of much of the land partially explains why the new intensification in agriculture which spread in most other European countries did not work in Spain. Peasant poverty, conservatism, and suspicion explain the rest.

5. Fortuitous

It was pure chance that Spain, in 1492, was introduced by Columbus to the heady atmosphere of the New World, at the very moment when the *Reconquista* had just been completed and a united Spain was ready to take her place in the political scene of Europe. (Columbus had been turned down at the courts of England and Portugal, the two countries which by all the rules ought to have invested in him.)

And when Spain, on the loss of her great American Empire, turned back to Europe, she was drained of energy, talent, and self-respect.

It was sheer bad luck that Ferdinand VII left a daughter to succeed him in 1833 instead of a son.

6. Religious

Because of Spain's traditional role as the bastion of South-Western Europe against the Moors, and the seven-hundred year Holy War—the *Reconquista*—the Church held a privileged and unique position over and above its status in any other country.

Its intolerance, its conservatism, its ubiquity, all had a stultifying effect on the development of education, liberalism, and the spirit of inquiry. The last victim of the Inquisition, for instance, was burnt as late as 1780.

7. Personal

>With the exception of Charles III, Spain's line of monarchs was uniformly poor, from the cretinous Charles II to the untrustworthy Ferdinand VII, who is beaten to the title 'worst king in Europe' only by his odious namesake on the throne of Naples.

>Many of those who struggled for power in Spain put the interests of Spain a very bad second, from Elizabeth Farnese and Alberoni to Godoy and Don Carlos.

>In the period under discussion, Spain did not produce one personality of European stature, except possibly Goya. And is it coincidence that it took the heroic War of Independence to produce the country's greatest painter since Murillo and Velasquez?

All that, of course, is very general. You still need to study rather more closely topics like:

1. The effects of the 'enlightened despotism' of Charles III (1759–88).

2. The repercussions in the Iberian peninsula of the French Revolution.

3. The reign of Charles IV:

   the involvement in the First Coalition.

   the tragic alliance with France.

   the War of Independence.

   the famous Constitution of 1812, which became a watchword and slogan for so many years to come.

4. The reign of Ferdinand VII:

   the aftermath of war.

   the rising of 1820.

   the succession of Isabella.

   the revolt of the South American colonies.

5. The growth of various factions:

    the Moderates

    the Progressives

    the Carlists

    the Republicans

    and the disputes and wars between them during the ill-starred reign of Isabella (1833–68).

6. The Revolution of 1868.

7. The brief reign of Amadeo.

8. The even briefer life of the First Republic.

9. The return of the Bourbons and a renewed attempt at constitutional monarchy.

One or two final speculations on Spain's eclipse:

(i) The axis of commercial power, which had shifted at the end of the Middle Ages from Central Europe to the Atlantic seaboard, was, due to nineteenth-century industrialism, shifting again—if not back east, at any rate north, away from Spain.

(ii) The late eighteenth and nineteenth century saw central Spain lose its dominating position. Peripheral Spain—Galicia, the Basque provinces, Catalonia—benefited; and regionalism, epitomised by the Carlist Wars, became powerful again.

(iii) Spain was unable to become a great power in either of the nineteenth-century ways:

    she had not the industry and resources to enable a dictator to play the power game like Louis Napoleon or Bismarck.

    she had not enough middle-class political experience or liberal tradition to produce healthy constitutional development along the lines of Britain.

(iv) The trouble lay in the Spanish character:

> centuries of Moorish domination had shown that the earthly life was worth living for its own sake, not as a Spartan, energetic preparation for the next.

> more centuries of South American wealth, with its by-products of indolent power and superior status (compare the British in India) had produced not merely *rois fainéants* but a whole *noblesse fainéante*.

> decades of civil strife, selfish rulers, and broken promises had evolved contemptuous apathy for politics.

> all that, plus the enervating heat, resulted in the engaging philosophy of *mañana*.

N.B. Whatever you do, don't transfer these ideas obediently to your notebooks. Consider them, criticise them, pull them to pieces; do not blindly accept them.
This applies equally to all the suggestions, speculations, observations, and generalisations put forward throughout this book.

Reading list

R. ALTAMIRA, *A History of Spain*, Van Norstrand, 1949.
W. C. ATKINSON, *A History of Spain and Portugal*, Pelican, 1967.
R. CARR, *Spain, 1808–1939*, Oxford, 1966.
S. DE MADARIAGA, *Spain: a Modern History*, Cape, 1961.
W. S. ROBERTSON, *The Rise of the Latin American Republics*, Collier-Macmillan, 1965.

General Reading list

Cambridge Modern History, Vols. IX, X.

A. BULLOCK and A. J. P. TAYLOR, *Select List of Books on European History, 1815–1914*, Revised 1957.

J. ROACH, *A Bibliography of Modern History*, Cambridge, 1968.

A. BIRNIE, *An Economic History of Europe, 1760–1939*, Methuen, Revised 1951.

J. BLUM
R. CAMERON } *The European World since 1815; Triumph and Transition*, Routledge, 1967.
T. G. BARNES

J. BOWLE, *Politics and Opinion in the Nineteenth Century*, Cape, 1954.

G. BRUUN, *Europe and the French Imperium*, Harper & Row, 1969.

H. A. L. FISHER, *History of Europe*, Arnold, 1936.

A. J. GRANT and H. TEMPERLEY, *Europe in the Nineteenth and Twentieth Centuries*, Sixth Edition, Longmans, 1952.

L. C. A. KNOWLES, *Economic Development in the Nineteenth Century —France, Germany, Russia and the United States*, Routledge, 1932.

E. LIPSON, *Europe in the Nineteenth Century*, Black, 1961.

J. MCMANNERS, *European History, 1789–1914: Men, Machines and Freedom*, Blackwell, 1966.

J. A. R. MARRIOTT, *Europe since Waterloo*, Methuen, 1931.

L. NAMIER, *Conflicts*, Macmillan, 1942.

L. NAMIER, *Vanished Supremacies*, Peregrine, 1962.

L. C. B. SEAMAN, *Vienna to Versailles*, Methuen, 1955.

P. N. STEARNS, *European Society in Upheaval: Social History since 1800*, Collier-Macmillan, 1967.

A. J. P. TAYLOR, *Grandeur and Decline*, Pelican, 1967.

D. THOMSON, *Europe since Napoleon*, Longmans, 1957.

E. L. WOODWARD, *Three Studies in European Conservatism*, Cass, 1963.

E. L. WOODWARD, *War and Peace in Europe, 1815–1870*, Cass, 1963.